INSTANT POT DUO CRISP AIR FRYER COOKBOOK

Easy and Delicious Recipes for Busy Lifestyles You'll Love Every Day

LOIS .B. POOLE

Copyright © 2024 By LOIS .B. POOLE. All rights reserved worldwide.

No part of this book may be reproduced or transmitted in any form or by any means, electronic or mechanical, including photocopying, recording, or by any information storage and retrieval system, without written permission from the publisher, except for the inclusion of brief quotations in a review.

Warning-Disclaimer:

The purpose of this book is to educate and entertain. The author or publisher does not guarantee that anyone following the techniques, suggestions, tips, ideas, or strategies will become successful. The author and publisher shall have neither liability nor responsibility to anyone with respect to any loss or damage caused, or alleged to be caused, directly or indirectly, by the information contained in this book.

This copyright notice and disclaimer apply to the entirety of the book and its contents, whether in print or electronic form, and extend to all future editions or revisions of the book. Unauthorized use or reproduction of this book or its contents is strictly prohibited and may result in legal action.

TABLE OF CONTENTS

INTRODUCTION TO INSTANT POT DUO CRISP AIR FRYER .7
- Overview of the Instant Pot Duo Crisp Air Fryer 7
- Benefits and Features of the Instant Pot Duo Crisp 8
- Tips for Using the Air Fryer Function Effectively 9

GETTING STARTED WITH INSTANT POT DUO CRISP 10
- Essential Instant Pot Duo Crisp Accessories 11

APPETIZERS AND SNACKS 14
1. Crispy Loaded Potato Skins 14
2. Spicy Air Fried Jalapeño Poppers 14
3. Cheesy Air Fried Quesadilla 15
4. Air Fried Pigs in a Blanket 16
5. Crispy Air Fried Egg Rolls 16
6. Flavorful Air Fried Samosas 17
7. Crunchy Air Fried Spring Rolls 18
8. Crispy Air Fried Chicken Nuggets 19
9. Crispy Air Fried Buffalo Cauliflower Bites 20
10. Crunchy Air Fried Coconut Shrimp 21
11. Crispy Air Fried Fried Pickles 21
12. Crispy Air Fried Fried Green Tomatoes 22
13. Crispy Air Fried Fried Zucchini 23
14. Crispy Air Fried Fried Mushrooms 23
15. Crunchy Air Fried Fried Cheese Curds 24

BREAKFASTS 25
1. Fluffy Air Fried Pancakes 25
2. Crispy Air Fried Waffles 26
3. Air Fried French Toast Sticks 27
4. Air Fried Hash Browns 27
5. Air Fried Breakfast Potatoes 28

6. Air Fried Bacon 29

7. Air Fried Sausages 29

8. Air Fried Breakfast Burritos 29

9. Air Fried Breakfast Sandwiches 30

10. Air Fried Omelets 31

11. Air Fried Frittatas 31

12. Air Fried Quiche 32

13. Air Fried Cinnamon Rolls 33

14. Air Fried Donuts 33

15. Air Fried Granola 34

CHICKEN MAIN DISHES 34

1. Air Fried Chicken Tenders 34

2. Air Fried Chicken Wings 35

3. Air Fried Chicken Drumsticks 36

4. Air Fried Chicken Thighs 36

5. Air Fried Chicken Breasts 37

6. Air Fried Chicken Parmesan 37

7. Air Fried Buffalo Chicken 38

8. Air Fried Fried Chicken 39

9. Air Fried Chicken Fajitas 39

10. Air Fried Chicken Tacos 40

11. Air Fried Chicken Enchiladas 41

12. Air Fried Chicken Pot Pie 41

13. Air Fried Chicken Marsala 42

14. Air Fried Chicken Cordon Bleu 43

15. Air Fried Chicken Piccata 43

BEEF MAIN DISHES 44

1. Air Fried Beef Jerky 44

2. Air Fried Steak Bites 45

3. Air Fried Steak Fajitas 46

4. Air Fried Steak Tacos 46

5. Air Fried Steak and Potatoes 47
6. Air Fried Cheesesteak 48
7. Air Fried Beef Empanadas 48
8. Air Fried Roast Beef 49
9. Air Fried Meatloaf 50
10. Air Fried Beef Wellington 51
11. Air Fried Beef Bourguignon 52
12. Air Fried Beef Stroganoff 53
13. Air Fried Mongolian Beef 54
14. Air Fried Beef Rouladen 55
15. Air Fried Salisbury Steak 56

PORK AND LAMB MAIN DISHES 57

1. Air Fried Pork Chops 57
2. Air Fried Baby Back Ribs 57
3. Air Fried Pork Carnitas 58
4. Air Fried Pork Fajitas 59
5. Air Fried Pulled Pork 59
6. Air Fried Bacon Wrapped Pork Tenderloin 60
7. Air Fried Sausage and Peppers 61
8. Air Fried Lamb Chops 62
9. Air Fried Lamb Kofta 62
10. Air Fried Lamb Souvlaki 63
11. Air Fried Lamb Meatballs 64
12. Air Fried Pork Satay 64
13. Air Fried Porchetta 65
14. Air Fried Pork Banh Mi 66

SEAFOOD MAIN DISHES 67

Air Fried Shrimp 67
Air Fried Fish Sticks 67
Air Fried Fish Tacos 68
Air Fried Coconut Shrimp 69

Air Fried Crab Cakes 70

Air Fried Fried Calamari 71

Air Fried Fried Catfish 72

Air Fried Fried Cod 72

Air Fried Fried Halibut 73

Air Fried Salmon 74

Air Fried Tuna Steaks 75

Air Fried Scallops 75

Air Fried Lobster Tails 76

Air Fried Oysters 77

Air Fried Fish and Chips 77

SIDE DISHES 78

Air Fried Mashed Potatoes 78

Air Fried Baked Potatoes 79

Air Fried Sweet Potato Casserole 80

Air Fried Potato Gratin 80

Air Fried Roasted Vegetables 81

Air Fried Roasted Potatoes 82

Air Fried French Fries 82

Air Fried Sweet Potato Fries 83

Air Fried Onion Rings 84

Air Fried Fried Okra 84

Air Fried Fried Green Tomatoes 85

Air Fried Brussels Sprouts 85

Air Fried Fried Cauliflower 86

Air Fried Fried Zucchini 87

Air Fried Fried Eggplant 87

DESSERTS 88

1. Air Fried Fruit Crisps 88

2. Air Fried Apple Pie 89

3. Air Fried Cheesecake 90

4. Air Fried Brownies 91
5. Air Fried Cookies 91
6. Air Fried Donuts 92
7. Air Fried Churros 93
8. Air Fried Fried Oreos 93
9. Air Fried Beignets 94
10. Air Fried Apple Fritters 95
11. Air Fried S'mores 96
12. Air Fried Bananas Foster 96
13. Air Fried Peach Cobbler 97
14. Air Fried Cinnamon Rolls 98

CLEANING AND MAINTAINING YOUR AIR FRYER 99
CONCLUSION 103

INTRODUCTION TO INSTANT POT DUO CRISP AIR FRYER

As an avid home cook, I'm always on the lookout for kitchen appliances and gadgets that can streamline the cooking process and help me get delicious, nutritious meals on the table faster. When the Instant Pot Duo Crisp first hit the market, I was immediately intrigued. The idea of having the combined power of a pressure cooker and an air fryer in one compact unit was truly revolutionary.

I've been using pressure cookers for years, and I've come to rely on them for their ability to drastically reduce cooking times while tenderizing even the toughest cuts of meat. But the one thing they've always lacked is the ability to achieve that signature crispy, golden-brown texture that you get from deep frying or oven roasting. That's where the air fryer lid on the Duo Crisp comes in.

With the simple switch from the pressure cooking lid to the air fryer lid, you can take your dishes to the next level. Suddenly, you can pressure cook foods to tender perfection, then finish them off in the air fryer for an irresistible crispy crust. No more separate pots and pans, no more monitoring multiple appliances - the Duo Crisp does it all in one convenient package.

But the Instant Pot Duo Crisp is so much more than just a pressure cooker and air fryer mashup. It's a 9-in-1 multicooker that can also sauté, steam, slow cook, sous vide, warm, bake, and roast. It's essentially replaced half a dozen appliances in my kitchen, freeing up valuable counter space and simplifying my cooking routine.

What I love most about the Duo Crisp is its sheer versatility. Whether I'm whipping up a batch of crispy air-fried chicken wings for game day, tender pressure-cooked beef stew for a cozy winter meal, or even baking up a batch of air-fried donuts for weekend brunch, this machine handles it all with ease. And the fact that it produces such consistently delicious results is the icing on the cake.

Of course, as with any new kitchen appliance, there's a bit of a learning curve when it comes to mastering the Duo Crisp. But Instant Brands has made it incredibly user-friendly, with intuitive pre-programmed settings and a clear, easy-to-read control panel. The included accessories, like the stainless steel steam rack and air fryer basket, also expand the appliance's functionality and make it a breeze to cook a wide variety of dishes.

In this cookbook, I'll share my favorite Instant Pot Duo Crisp recipes, from crowd-pleasing appetizers to hearty main courses and sweet treats. But before we dive into the recipes, I want to give you a comprehensive overview of this amazing appliance - its key features, the benefits it offers, and some tips and techniques for getting the most out of the air fryer function.

Whether you're a seasoned pressure cooker pro or new to the world of multicookers, I'm confident that the Instant Pot Duo Crisp will revolutionize the way you approach meal prep and cooking at home. So let's get started!

OVERVIEW OF THE INSTANT POT DUO CRISP AIR FRYER

When Instant Brands first introduced the Duo Crisp, I have to admit, I was a bit skeptical. After all, how could one appliance possibly replace my trusty pressure cooker, air fryer, slow cooker, and a handful of other kitchen gadgets? But after unboxing the Duo Crisp and giving it a try, I was completely won over. This truly is a game-changing, do-it-all kitchen tool.

The foundation of the Duo Crisp is the 8-quart stainless steel inner pot, which provides ample capacity for cooking family-sized meals or batch prepping ingredients for the week ahead. I love that the inner pot is made of high-quality stainless steel rather than a nonstick coating. It's durable, easy to clean, and creates beautifully even heat distribution for consistent cooking results.

But the real star of the show is the air fryer lid. With its powerful 1500-watt heating element and rapid air circulation system, this lid transforms the Duo Crisp into a next-level air fryer. The hot air gets circulated around your food at high speed, creating that signature crispy, golden-brown texture we all crave - no deep frying required.

What I find most impressive about the Duo Crisp's air frying capabilities is how evenly it cooks. There's no more dealing with unevenly cooked, soggy results or having to manually flip and rotate your food halfway through. The air fryer lid ensures everything gets that perfect air-fried finish, from french fries to chicken wings to even delicate items like fish fillets.

Of course, the Duo Crisp doesn't just excel at air frying - it's a true multicooker powerhouse. With 9 built-in smart programs, you can pressure cook, sauté, steam, slow cook, sous vide, warm, bake, roast, and yes, air fry all in the same compact appliance. It's like having an entire suite of kitchen gadgets condensed into one streamlined countertop unit.

One of my favorite features is the ability to seamlessly transition between pressure cooking and air frying. For example, I can pressure cook a tough cut of meat until it's fall-off-the-bone tender, then simply swap out the lids to crisp up the exterior in the air fryer. This two-in-one functionality is a total game-changer, saving me tons of time and effort compared to using separate appliances.

The included accessories also expand the Duo Crisp's versatility even further. The stainless steel steam rack is great for steaming delicate foods, the broiling/dehydrating tray is perfect for crisping up the top of casseroles or making healthy homemade jerky, and the multi-purpose rack allows you to cook on multiple levels. It's like having a fully-equipped kitchen in one compact countertop appliance.

Whether you're an experienced home chef or just starting to explore the world of multicookers, the Instant Pot Duo Crisp has so much to offer. With its unparalleled combination of pressure cooking and air frying power, not to mention all the other cooking functions, this appliance has quickly become the centerpiece of my kitchen. I can't wait to share all the delicious recipes and cooking tips I've discovered with you!

BENEFITS AND FEATURES OF THE INSTANT POT DUO CRISP

As someone who loves nothing more than discovering kitchen gadgets and appliances that can streamline my cooking process, the Instant Pot Duo Crisp has quickly become my new best friend. From the moment I unboxed this versatile multicooker, I was blown away by its incredible array of features and the myriad of benefits it offers.

Let's start with the game-changing 2-in-1 functionality. Having the ability to pressure cook and air fry all in one compact appliance is nothing short of revolutionary. No more juggling multiple pots, pans, and appliances - the Duo Crisp allows me to pressure cook a dish to tender perfection, then finish it off in the air fryer for a crispy, golden-brown crust, all without leaving my countertop. This seamless transition between cooking methods is a total time-saver and has eliminated so much cleanup for me.

But the Duo Crisp's versatility extends far beyond just pressure cooking and air frying. As a true 9-in-1 multicooker, this appliance can also sauté, steam, slow cook, sous vide, warm, bake, and roast. In essence, it's replaced at least half a dozen different kitchen gadgets for me, freeing up valuable counter space and consolidating my cooking process.

One of my favorite features of the Duo Crisp is its large 8-quart capacity. This generous size means I can easily cook family-sized portions or prepare big-batch recipes for meal prepping. Whether I'm air frying up a tray of crispy chicken wings for game day or pressure cooking a hearty beef stew to feed a crowd, the Duo Crisp's ample inner pot ensures I have plenty of room to work.

And speaking of air frying, the Duo Crisp's advanced heating and air circulation technology is truly impressive. The powerful 1500-watt heating element and rapid air flow ensure my foods get that signature air-fried crispiness, with none of the greasiness or uneven cooking that can sometimes plague traditional air fryers. I'm able to achieve restaurant-quality results at home, without the guilt of deep frying.

Another standout benefit of the Duo Crisp is how user-friendly and intuitive it is. The digital control panel with pre-programmed cooking settings takes all the guesswork out of pressure cooking, air frying, and the appliance's other functions. Even for a relative multicooker novice like myself, I was able to start churning out delicious, perfectly cooked meals right away, with no lengthy learning curve.

Of course, the Duo Crisp's benefits extend beyond just the kitchen. As a health-conscious home cook, I appreciate how the air frying function allows me to enjoy all the flavor and crunch of fried foods, but with a fraction of the fat and calories. And with the ability to batch cook and meal prep, I'm saving time, money, and reducing food waste in my household.

Ultimately, the Instant Pot Duo Crisp has proven to be an invaluable addition to my kitchen. Its unparalleled combination of pressure cooking and air frying power, along with its long list of other cooking functions, has streamlined my meal prep process and expanded the range of delicious, wholesome dishes I'm able to create at home. I can't recommend this multicooker highly enough for anyone looking to simplify their cooking routine.

TIPS FOR USING THE AIR FRYER FUNCTION EFFECTIVELY

As someone who has been using the Instant Pot Duo Crisp for several months now, I can attest that mastering the air fryer function takes a bit of practice. But once you get the hang of it, the results are absolutely worth it. Perfectly crispy, evenly cooked foods with a fraction of the oil and fat - what's not to love?

The first and most important tip I can offer is to make sure you preheat the air fryer lid before adding your food. Just like a traditional oven, taking the time to preheat ensures the Duo Crisp's heating element and fan are at the optimal temperature to deliver that signature air-fried crunch. I usually recommend preheating for 3-5 minutes before air frying.

Another key factor in achieving great air frying results is using the right amount of oil. While the beauty of air frying is that you need significantly less oil than traditional deep frying, a light coating can still help foods get extra crispy. I generally find that 1-2 teaspoons of oil per batch is the sweet spot - any more and you risk excess smoke, splatter, and an overly greasy final product.

When it comes to the food itself, it's important to cut everything into uniform, evenly sized pieces. This promotes even cooking throughout, ensuring all your ingredients reach that perfect level of crispness at the same time. No more dealing with some items being underdone while others are burnt to a crisp.

And speaking of even cooking, it's crucial not to overcrowd the air fryer basket. Leaving a little space between each piece of food allows the hot air to circulate freely and reach all surfaces. If you try to cram too much in at once, you'll end up with steamed, soggy results instead of that sought-after crispiness. Work in batches if needed to maintain a single, well-spaced layer.

To get the most out of your air frying, be sure to flip or toss your food halfway through the cooking time. This ensures all sides are evenly exposed to the hot air for optimum crispness. And if you want to take things to the next level, try using the broil function once your food is cooked through. The intense, direct heat will give you an extra golden-brown, restaurant-quality finish.

Of course, no discussion of air frying tips would be complete without mentioning the importance of proper cleaning and maintenance. After each use, be diligent about thoroughly cleaning the air fryer basket, tray, and all interior surfaces. Food debris and grease buildup can really hamper the Duo Crisp's performance over time. Refer to the manufacturer's instructions for the best cleaning methods.

Finally, don't be afraid to get creative and experiment with the air frying function. One of the best things about this technology is that it opens up a whole new world of cooking possibilities beyond just traditional fried foods. Try air frying vegetables, proteins, even desserts - the results might just surprise you.

With these tips in mind, you'll be well on your way to mastering air frying with your Instant Pot Duo Crisp. Crispy, crave-worthy results are just the push of a button away. Now let's dive into some delicious air fryer recipes!

GETTING STARTED WITH INSTANT POT DUO CRISP

When I first unboxed my Instant Pot Duo Crisp, I have to admit, I was a bit overwhelmed by all the different components and accessories. But after taking a few minutes to carefully inspect each piece, I quickly realized just how versatile and well-designed this multicooker really is.

The first thing you'll notice is the two distinct lids - the classic pressure cooking lid, and the newer air fryer lid. Both are essential for unlocking the full potential of the Duo Crisp. The pressure cooking lid allows you to take advantage of all the advanced pressure cooking features, while the air fryer lid transforms the Duo Crisp into a powerful convection oven for achieving that signature crispy texture.

Before you can start whipping up delicious air-fried and pressure-cooked meals, you'll need to give your new Duo Crisp a proper cleaning. This is an important step to ensure your appliance is in perfect working order and to remove any manufacturing residues. I always recommend washing all the removable parts in warm, soapy water.

Once everything is washed and dried, you can begin setting up your Duo Crisp on the countertop. But before diving straight into cooking, I highly recommend running an initial test run of your appliance. This will help you get familiar with the functions and ensure everything is in proper working order before you start preparing food.

Step-by-Step Guide on Setting Up and Using the Instant Pot Duo Crisp

After carefully unpacking my new Instant Pot Duo Crisp and giving all the components a thorough cleaning, I was eager to get this powerful multicooker set up and ready for action in my kitchen. As someone who loves efficiency and streamlined cooking, the idea of having both pressure cooking and air frying capabilities in a single appliance was incredibly appealing.

The first step in the setup process is finding the perfect spot for your Duo Crisp on the countertop. You'll want to choose a stable, level surface that's at least 5 inches away from any walls or other appliances. This clearance is essential to ensure proper air flow and ventilation, especially when using the air fryer lid.

Once you've selected the ideal location, it's time to place the stainless steel inner pot into the base of the Duo Crisp. This cooking pot is where all the magic happens, so you'll want to make sure it's securely positioned before moving on. Double-check that the exterior of the inner pot and the heating element inside the base are both clean and dry.

With the inner pot in place, you're ready to start your initial test run. This is a crucial step that I always recommend completing before the first use of your Duo Crisp. It only takes about 10 minutes, but it can give you invaluable peace of mind knowing your new appliance is set up correctly and ready to deliver consistent, safe cooking results.

To perform the test run, simply add 3 cups of water to the inner pot (no food necessary) and secure the pressure cooking lid, making sure the steam release valve is in the "Sealing" position. Then, select the "Pressure Cook" function and set the time for 3 minutes. This brief pressure cooking cycle will allow you to check that the lid is sealing properly and the inner pot is heating up as expected.

Once the 3 minutes are up, carefully use the quick release method to depressurize the Duo Crisp. This involves flipping the steam release valve to the "Venting" position to rapidly release any remaining steam and pressure. After the float valve has dropped down, indicating the pressure has fully released, you can open the lid and check that the water has heated through thoroughly.

The final step of the test run is to try out the air fryer lid. Place the lid on the Duo Crisp base and select the "Air Fry" function, setting the time for 5 minutes. Listen and watch for the heating element to activate, and check that the air is circulating as expected. When the cycle is complete, carefully remove the lid and ensure the heating element feels hot to the touch.

Performing this initial test run gives you the opportunity to get familiar with the Duo Crisp's controls and features before cooking any actual food. It also allows you to troubleshoot and address any potential issues right away, rather than discovering them mid-recipe. Trust me, taking these 10 minutes upfront will save you a lot of headaches down the road.

With the setup and test run complete, you're now ready to start exploring all the amazing cooking possibilities of your new Instant Pot Duo Crisp! Just remember to always consult the included instruction manual for detailed safety guidelines and usage tips. Bon appétit!

ESSENTIAL INSTANT POT DUO CRISP ACCESSORIES

While the Instant Pot Duo Crisp comes with a great selection of accessories right out of the box, there are a few additional items that can really elevate your cooking experience. Whether you're looking to expand your air frying capabilities, streamline your meal prep, or make cleanup a breeze, these essential accessories are worth considering.

Air Fryer Basket Liners

These perforated silicone mats or parchment paper liners are designed to fit perfectly in the air fryer basket. They help prevent sticking and make cleanup a cinch, especially for messy foods like chicken wings or fries. The silicone liners can be reused time and time again, while the parchment paper liners provide a disposable option that's great for quick cleanup. Both types of liners allow hot air to circulate around your food for even crisping, without the risk of your ingredients adhering to the basket.

Steamer Basket

A stainless steel steamer basket allows you to steam vegetables, seafood, and more above the liquid in the inner pot. This is a great way to cook multiple components of a meal at the same time, like tender-crisp broccoli alongside perfectly cooked salmon. The basket sits atop a trivet in the inner pot, keeping your delicate foods elevated and preventing them from sitting in the cooking liquid. Whether you're preparing a healthy one-pot dinner or just want to streamline your meal prep, a steamer basket is an essential accessory for the Instant Pot Duo Crisp.

Muffin Tin

Compact muffin tins, whether made of silicone or metal, work wonderfully in the air fryer lid. You can use them to bake up perfect individual portions of everything from egg bites and mini frittatas to bite-sized desserts. The tight spacing of the muffin cups helps ensure even cooking and browning, while the compact size makes them perfect for air frying. Plus, muffin tins are incredibly versatile - you can use them not just for baking, but also for steaming, poaching, and more.

Baking Trivet

A sturdy, oven-safe baking trivet can be used in the air fryer for baking, broiling, and even dehydrating. It provides an elevated surface to ensure even cooking by allowing hot air to circulate all around your food. Trivet accessories come in a variety of shapes and sizes to fit the Instant Pot's inner pot, and some even have built-in handles for easy removal. Whether you're making crispy chicken wings, dehydrated veggie chips, or broiled salmon, a baking trivet is an invaluable tool.

Silicone Mitts

Protecting your hands is crucial when dealing with the hot surfaces of the Instant Pot Duo Crisp. A good pair of silicone oven mitts will make handling the hot inner pot and air fryer lid a breeze. Look for mitts that are heat-resistant up to at least 400°F to ensure safe handling even when your appliance is at its maximum temperature. The long, secure cuffs will also help shield your forearms from any steam or splatter.

Cooking Thermometer

An instant-read meat thermometer is an essential accessory for ensuring your proteins are cooked to a safe internal temperature, especially when pressure cooking or air frying. With the Duo Crisp's ability to rapidly cook foods, a thermometer will take the guesswork out of determining when your dish is fully cooked through. This will help you achieve perfectly tender, juicy results every time.

Aside from these must-have accessories, you may also want to consider investing in items like a silicone basting brush, air fryer cleaning brush, and extra inner pots or air fryer baskets to streamline your workflow. Remember, the key to getting the most out of your Instant Pot Duo Crisp is having the right tools on hand. Take some time to explore the wide range of Instant Pot-approved accessories and find the ones that best fit your cooking needs and style.

APPETIZERS AND SNACKS

1. CRISPY LOADED POTATO SKINS

Prep: 15 mins | Cook: 30 mins | Serves: 4

Ingredients:

- 4 large russet potatoes (about 2 pounds), scrubbed and dried
- 1 tablespoon olive oil (UK: 15ml)
- Salt and pepper to taste
- 1 cup shredded cheddar cheese (UK: 100g)
- 4 slices cooked bacon, crumbled
- 2 green onions, thinly sliced
- Sour cream, for serving

Instructions:

1. Preheat the Instant Pot Duo Crisp Air Fryer lid to 400°F (200°C).
2. Slice each potato in half lengthwise. Scoop out the flesh, leaving about ¼ inch of potato attached to the skin.
3. Brush the inside and outside of the potato skins with olive oil. Season with salt and pepper.
4. Place the potato skins in the air fryer basket, skin side down. Air fry for 15 minutes.
5. Remove the basket and fill each skin with shredded cheese and bacon.
6. Return the basket to the air fryer and cook for an additional 5-7 minutes, or until the cheese is melted and bubbly.
7. Sprinkle with sliced green onions and serve with sour cream on the side.

Nutritional Info: Calories: 320 | Fat: 18g | Carbs: 27g | Protein: 14g

Instant Pot Duo Crisp Air Fryer Functions Used: Air Fryer

2. SPICY AIR FRIED JALAPEÑO POPPERS

Prep: 20 mins | Cook: 10 mins | Serves: 6

Ingredients:

- 12 large jalapeño peppers
- 8 ounces cream cheese, softened (UK: 225g)
- 1 cup shredded cheddar cheese (UK: 100g)
- 1 teaspoon garlic powder (UK: 5ml)
- 1 teaspoon onion powder (UK: 5ml)
- Salt and pepper to taste

- ½ cup breadcrumbs (UK: 50g)

- Cooking spray

Instructions:

1. Preheat the Instant Pot Duo Crisp Air Fryer lid to 375°F (190°C).

2. Cut the jalapeños in half lengthwise and remove the seeds and membranes.

3. In a bowl, mix together the cream cheese, cheddar cheese, garlic powder, onion powder, salt, and pepper.

4. Stuff each jalapeño half with the cheese mixture.

5. Place the breadcrumbs in a shallow dish. Coat each stuffed jalapeño with breadcrumbs.

6. Spray the air fryer basket with cooking spray. Arrange the jalapeños in a single layer in the basket.

7. Air fry for 8-10 minutes, or until the jalapeños are golden brown and crispy.

8. Serve hot with your favorite dipping sauce.

Nutritional Info: Calories: 180 | Fat: 12g | Carbs: 12g | Protein: 7g

Instant Pot Duo Crisp Air Fryer Functions Used: Air Fryer

3. CHEESY AIR FRIED QUESADILLA

Prep: 10 mins | Cook: 10 mins | Serves: 2

Ingredients:

- 2 large flour tortillas

- 1 cup shredded cheese (such as cheddar or Monterey Jack) (UK: 100g)

- ¼ cup diced bell peppers (UK: 30g)

- ¼ cup diced onions (UK: 30g)

- 2 tablespoons chopped fresh cilantro (UK: 30ml)

- Cooking spray

Instructions:

1. Preheat the Instant Pot Duo Crisp Air Fryer lid to 375°F (190°C).

2. Place one tortilla on a flat surface. Sprinkle half of the cheese evenly over the tortilla.

3. Top with diced bell peppers, onions, and chopped cilantro.

4. Sprinkle the remaining cheese over the toppings.

5. Place the second tortilla on top and press down gently.

6. Spray both sides of the quesadilla with cooking spray.

7. Carefully transfer the quesadilla to the air fryer basket.

8. Air fry for 5 minutes, then flip the quesadilla and air fry for an additional 5 minutes, or until crispy and golden brown.

9. Remove from the air fryer and cut into wedges.

10. Serve hot with salsa and sour cream.

Nutritional Info: Calories: 350 | Fat: 18g | Carbs: 30g | Protein: 15g

Instant Pot Duo Crisp Air Fryer Functions Used: Air Fryer

4. AIR FRIED PIGS IN A BLANKET

Prep: 15 mins | Cook: 12 mins | Serves: 8

Ingredients:

- 1 can refrigerated crescent roll dough

- 32 cocktail sausages

- Ketchup and mustard, for serving

Instructions:

1. Preheat the Instant Pot Duo Crisp Air Fryer lid to 375°F (190°C).

2. Unroll the crescent roll dough and cut each triangle into two smaller triangles.

3. Wrap each cocktail sausage with a piece of dough, leaving the ends exposed to resemble "pigs in a blanket".

4. Place the wrapped sausages in a single layer in the air fryer basket.

5. Air fry for 10-12 minutes, or until the dough is golden brown and cooked through.

6. Serve hot with ketchup and mustard for dipping.

Nutritional Info: Calories: 150 | Fat: 10g | Carbs: 10g | Protein: 5g

Instant Pot Duo Crisp Air Fryer Functions Used: Air Fryer

5. CRISPY AIR FRIED EGG ROLLS

Prep: 20 mins | Cook: 15 mins | Serves: 4

Ingredients:

- 8 egg roll wrappers

- 1 cup shredded cabbage (UK: 100g)

- 1 cup shredded carrots (UK: 100g)

- ½ cup finely chopped cooked chicken (UK: 50g)

- 2 tablespoons soy sauce (UK: 30ml)

- 1 tablespoon sesame oil (UK: 15ml)

- 1 teaspoon minced garlic (UK: 5ml)

- 1 teaspoon minced ginger (UK: 5ml)

- Cooking spray

- Sweet chili sauce, for serving

Instructions:

1. Preheat the Instant Pot Duo Crisp Air Fryer lid to 375°F (190°C).

2. In a bowl, mix together the shredded cabbage, shredded carrots, cooked chicken, soy sauce, sesame oil, minced garlic, and minced ginger until well combined.

3. Lay an egg roll wrapper on a clean surface with one corner pointing toward you.

4. Place about 2 tablespoons of the filling in the center of the wrapper.

5. Fold the bottom corner over the filling, then fold in the sides, and roll it up tightly.

6. Seal the edge with a dab of water.

7. Repeat with the remaining wrappers and filling.

8. Spray the egg rolls with cooking spray.

9. Place them in the air fryer basket in a single layer, seam side down.

10. Air fry for 12-15 minutes, or until golden brown and crispy, turning halfway through.

11. Serve hot with sweet chili sauce for dipping.

Nutritional Info: Calories: 180 | Fat: 6g | Carbs: 25g | Protein: 8g

Instant Pot Duo Crisp Air Fryer Functions Used: Air Fryer

6. FLAVORFUL AIR FRIED SAMOSAS

Prep: 30 mins | Cook: 20 mins | Serves: 6

Ingredients:

- 2 cups mashed potatoes (UK: 450g)

- 1 cup frozen peas, thawed (UK: 100g)

- 1 small onion, finely chopped (UK: 1)

- 2 cloves garlic, minced (UK: 2)

- 1 teaspoon grated ginger (UK: 5ml)

- 1 teaspoon ground cumin (UK: 5ml)

- 1 teaspoon ground coriander (UK: 5ml)

- ½ teaspoon turmeric powder (UK: 2.5ml)

- Salt and pepper, to taste

- 2 tablespoons chopped fresh cilantro (UK: 30ml)

- 12 sheets phyllo pastry, thawed

- Cooking spray

- Mango chutney, for serving

Instructions:

1. Preheat the Instant Pot Duo Crisp Air Fryer lid to 375°F (190°C).

2. In a large bowl, mix together the mashed potatoes, peas, chopped onion, minced garlic, grated ginger, ground cumin, ground coriander, turmeric powder, salt, pepper, and chopped cilantro until well combined.

3. Lay one sheet of phyllo pastry on a clean surface and brush lightly with cooking spray.

4. Fold the sheet in half lengthwise.

5. Place a spoonful of the potato filling at one end of the strip.

6. Fold the pastry over the filling to form a triangle, then continue folding diagonally until you reach the end of the strip.

7. Seal the edges with a dab of water.

8. Repeat with the remaining pastry sheets and filling.

9. Spray the samosas with cooking spray.

10. Place them in the air fryer basket in a single layer.

11. Air fry for 18-20 minutes, or until golden brown and crispy, turning halfway through.

12. Serve hot with mango chutney on the side.

Nutritional Info: Calories: 220 | Fat: 5g | Carbs: 40g | Protein: 5g

Instant Pot Duo Crisp Air Fryer Functions Used: Air Fryer

7. CRUNCHY AIR FRIED SPRING ROLLS

Prep: 25 mins | Cook: 15 mins | Serves: 4

Ingredients:

- 8 spring roll wrappers
- 1 cup shredded cabbage (UK: 100g)
- 1 cup shredded carrots (UK: 100g)
- 1 cup bean sprouts (UK: 100g)
- ½ cup cooked vermicelli noodles (UK: 50g)
- 2 tablespoons soy sauce (UK: 30ml)
- 1 tablespoon sesame oil (UK: 15ml)
- 1 teaspoon minced garlic (UK: 5ml)
- 1 teaspoon minced ginger (UK: 5ml)
- Cooking spray
- Sweet chili sauce, for dipping

Instructions:

1. Preheat the Instant Pot Duo Crisp Air Fryer lid to 375°F (190°C).

2. In a bowl, combine the shredded cabbage, shredded carrots, bean sprouts, cooked vermicelli noodles, soy sauce, sesame oil, minced garlic, and minced ginger.

3. Place a spring roll wrapper on a clean surface with one corner pointing toward you.

4. Spoon about 2 tablespoons of the filling onto the bottom third of the wrapper.

5. Fold the bottom corner over the filling, then fold in the sides, and roll it up tightly.

6. Seal the edge with a dab of water.

7. Repeat with the remaining wrappers and filling.

8. Spray the spring rolls with cooking spray.

9. Place them in the air fryer basket in a single layer, seam side down.

10. Air fry for 12-15 minutes, or until golden brown and crispy, turning halfway through.

11. Serve hot with sweet chili sauce for dipping.

Nutritional Info: Calories: 160 | Fat: 3g | Carbs: 28g | Protein: 5g

Instant Pot Duo Crisp Air Fryer Functions Used: Air Fryer

8. CRISPY AIR FRIED CHICKEN NUGGETS

Prep: 20 mins | Cook: 15 mins | Serves: 4

Ingredients:

- 1 lb boneless, skinless chicken breasts, cut into bite-sized pieces (UK: 450g)

- 1 cup all-purpose flour (UK: 120g)

- 2 eggs, beaten (UK: 2)

- 1 cup breadcrumbs (UK: 100g)

- 1 teaspoon garlic powder (UK: 5ml)

- 1 teaspoon onion powder (UK: 5ml)

- 1 teaspoon paprika (UK: 5ml)

- 1 teaspoon salt (UK: 5ml)

- Cooking spray

- Honey mustard sauce, for dipping

Instructions:

1. Preheat the Instant Pot Duo Crisp Air Fryer lid to 375°F (190°C).

2. Set up a breading station with three shallow bowls: one with flour, one with beaten eggs, and one with breadcrumbs mixed with garlic powder, onion powder, paprika, and salt.

3. Dip each chicken piece into the flour, shaking off any excess.

4. Dip the chicken into the beaten eggs, then coat with the breadcrumb mixture, pressing gently to adhere.

5. Place the breaded chicken nuggets in a single layer in the air fryer basket.

6. Spray the nuggets with cooking spray.

7. Air fry for 12-15 minutes, or until golden brown and cooked through, flipping halfway through.

8. Serve hot with honey mustard sauce for dipping.

Nutritional Info: Calories: 280 | Fat: 8g | Carbs: 27g | Protein: 23g

Instant Pot Duo Crisp Air Fryer Functions Used: Air Fryer

9. CRISPY AIR FRIED BUFFALO CAULIFLOWER BITES

Prep: 15 mins | Cook: 20 mins | Serves: 4

Ingredients:

- 1 head cauliflower, cut into florets (UK: 1 medium cauliflower)
- ½ cup all-purpose flour (UK: 60g)
- ½ cup water (UK: 120ml)
- 1 teaspoon garlic powder (UK: 5ml)
- 1 teaspoon onion powder (UK: 5ml)
- ½ teaspoon salt (UK: 2.5ml)
- ½ teaspoon black pepper (UK: 2.5ml)
- ½ cup buffalo sauce (UK: 120ml)
- 2 tablespoons melted butter (UK: 30g)
- Cooking spray
- Ranch or blue cheese dressing, for dipping

Instructions:

1. Preheat the Instant Pot Duo Crisp Air Fryer lid to 375°F (190°C).

2. In a bowl, whisk together the flour, water, garlic powder, onion powder, salt, and black pepper to make the batter.

3. Dip each cauliflower floret into the batter, shaking off any excess.

4. Place the coated cauliflower florets in a single layer in the air fryer basket.

5. Spray the cauliflower with cooking spray.

6. Air fry for 18-20 minutes, or until golden brown and crispy.

7. In a separate bowl, mix together the buffalo sauce and melted butter.

8. Toss the air fried cauliflower in the buffalo sauce mixture until evenly coated.

9. Serve hot with ranch or blue cheese dressing for dipping.

Nutritional Info: Calories: 140 | Fat: 6g | Carbs: 19g | Protein: 4g

Instant Pot Duo Crisp Air Fryer Functions Used: Air Fryer

10. CRUNCHY AIR FRIED COCONUT SHRIMP

Prep: 20 mins | Cook: 10 mins | Serves: 4

Ingredients:

- 1 lb large shrimp, peeled and deveined (UK: 450g)

- ½ cup all-purpose flour (UK: 60g)

- 2 eggs, beaten (UK: 2)

- 1 cup sweetened shredded coconut (UK: 100g)

- ½ cup Panko breadcrumbs (UK: 50g)

- Cooking spray

- Sweet chili sauce, for dipping

Instructions:

1. Preheat the Instant Pot Duo Crisp Air Fryer lid to 375°F (190°C).

2. Set up a breading station with three shallow bowls: one with flour, one with beaten eggs, and one with a mixture of sweetened shredded coconut and Panko breadcrumbs.

3. Dip each shrimp into the flour, then the beaten eggs, and finally coat with the coconut breadcrumb mixture, pressing gently to adhere.

4. Place the breaded shrimp in a single layer in the air fryer basket.

5. Spray the shrimp with cooking spray.

6. Air fry for 8-10 minutes, or until golden brown and crispy, flipping halfway through.

7. Serve hot with sweet chili sauce for dipping.

Nutritional Info: Calories: 250 | Fat: 10g | Carbs: 24g | Protein: 16g

Instant Pot Duo Crisp Air Fryer Functions Used: Air Fryer

11. CRISPY AIR FRIED FRIED PICKLES

Prep: 15 mins | Cook: 10 mins | Serves: 4

Ingredients:

- 1 jar dill pickle chips, drained (UK: 1 jar of pickled gherkins)

- 1 cup all-purpose flour (UK: 120g)

- 2 eggs, beaten (UK: 2)

- 1 cup Panko breadcrumbs (UK: 100g)

- 1 teaspoon garlic powder (UK: 5ml)

- 1 teaspoon paprika (UK: 5ml)
- Cooking spray
- Ranch dressing, for dipping

Instructions:

1. Preheat the Instant Pot Duo Crisp Air Fryer lid to 375°F (190°C).

2. Set up a breading station with three shallow bowls: one with flour, one with beaten eggs, and one with Panko breadcrumbs mixed with garlic powder and paprika.

3. Dip each pickle chip into the flour, then the beaten eggs, and finally coat with the seasoned Panko breadcrumbs, pressing gently to adhere.

4. Place the breaded pickle chips in a single layer in the air fryer basket.

5. Spray the pickle chips with cooking spray.

6. Air fry for 8-10 minutes, or until golden brown and crispy, flipping halfway through.

7. Serve hot with ranch dressing for dipping.

Nutritional Info: Calories: 180 | Fat: 3g | Carbs: 31g | Protein: 6g

Instant Pot Duo Crisp Air Fryer Functions Used: Air Fryer

12. CRISPY AIR FRIED FRIED GREEN TOMATOES

Prep: 15 mins | Cook: 15 mins | Serves: 4

Ingredients:

- 2 large green tomatoes, sliced into ¼-inch rounds (UK: 2 large green tomatoes)
- 1 cup all-purpose flour (UK: 120g)
- 2 eggs, beaten (UK: 2)
- 1 cup Panko breadcrumbs (UK: 100g)
- 1 teaspoon garlic powder (UK: 5ml)
- 1 teaspoon paprika (UK: 5ml)
- Cooking spray
- Salt and pepper, to taste

Instructions:

1. Preheat the Instant Pot Duo Crisp Air Fryer lid to 375°F (190°C).

2. Set up a breading station with three shallow bowls: one with flour, one with beaten eggs, and one with Panko breadcrumbs mixed with garlic powder and paprika.

3. Dip each tomato slice into the flour, then the beaten eggs, and finally coat with the seasoned Panko breadcrumbs, pressing gently to adhere.

4. Place the breaded tomato slices in a single layer in the air fryer basket.

5. Spray the tomato slices with cooking spray and season with salt and pepper.

6. Air fry for 12-15 minutes, or until golden brown and crispy, flipping halfway through.

7. Serve hot as a side dish or appetizer.

Nutritional Info: Calories: 160 | Fat: 2g | Carbs: 29g | Protein: 7g

Instant Pot Duo Crisp Air Fryer Functions Used: Air Fryer

13. CRISPY AIR FRIED FRIED ZUCCHINI

Prep: 15 mins | Cook: 10 mins | Serves: 4

Ingredients:

- 2 medium zucchinis, sliced into ¼-inch rounds (UK: 2 medium courgettes)

- 1 cup all-purpose flour (UK: 120g)

- 2 eggs, beaten (UK: 2)

- 1 cup Panko breadcrumbs (UK: 100g)

- 1 teaspoon garlic powder (UK: 5ml)

- 1 teaspoon Italian seasoning (UK: 5ml)

- Cooking spray

- Marinara sauce, for dipping

Instructions:

1. Preheat the Instant Pot Duo Crisp Air Fryer lid to 375°F (190°C).

2. Set up a breading station with three shallow bowls: one with flour, one with beaten eggs, and one with Panko breadcrumbs mixed with garlic powder and Italian seasoning.

3. Dip each zucchini slice into the flour, then the beaten eggs, and finally coat with the seasoned Panko breadcrumbs, pressing gently to adhere.

4. Place the breaded zucchini slices in a single layer in the air fryer basket.

5. Spray the zucchini slices with cooking spray.

6. Air fry for 8-10 minutes, or until golden brown and crispy, flipping halfway through.

7. Serve hot with marinara sauce for dipping.

Nutritional Info: Calories: 170 | Fat: 2g | Carbs: 31g | Protein: 8g

Instant Pot Duo Crisp Air Fryer Functions Used: Air Fryer

14. CRISPY AIR FRIED FRIED MUSHROOMS

Prep: 15 mins | Cook: 10 mins | Serves: 4

Ingredients:

- 1 pound button mushrooms, cleaned (UK: 450g)

- 1 cup all-purpose flour (UK: 120g)

- 2 eggs, beaten (UK: 2)

- 1 cup Panko breadcrumbs (UK: 100g)

- 1 teaspoon garlic powder (UK: 5ml)

- 1 teaspoon dried parsley (UK: 5ml)

- Cooking spray

- Garlic aioli, for dipping

Instructions:

1. Preheat the Instant Pot Duo Crisp Air Fryer lid to 375°F (190°C).

2. Set up a breading station with three shallow bowls: one with flour, one with beaten eggs, and one with Panko breadcrumbs mixed with garlic powder and dried parsley.

3. Dip each mushroom into the flour, then the beaten eggs, and finally coat with the seasoned Panko breadcrumbs, pressing gently to adhere.

4. Place the breaded mushrooms in a single layer in the air fryer basket.

5. Spray the mushrooms with cooking spray.

6. Air fry for 8-10 minutes, or until golden brown and crispy, flipping halfway through.

7. Serve hot with garlic aioli for dipping.

Nutritional Info: Calories: 160 | Fat: 3g | Carbs: 27g | Protein: 8g

Instant Pot Duo Crisp Air Fryer Functions Used: Air Fryer

15. CRUNCHY AIR FRIED FRIED CHEESE CURDS

Prep: 10 mins | Cook: 8 mins | Serves: 4

Ingredients:

- 1 cup cheese curds (UK: 100g)

- 1 cup all-purpose flour (UK: 120g)

- 2 eggs, beaten (UK: 2)

- 1 cup Panko breadcrumbs (UK: 100g)

- 1 teaspoon paprika (UK: 5ml)

- 1 teaspoon onion powder (UK: 5ml)

- Cooking spray

- Marinara sauce, for dipping

Instructions:

1. Preheat the Instant Pot Duo Crisp Air Fryer lid to 375°F (190°C).

2. Set up a breading station with three shallow bowls: one with flour, one with beaten eggs, and one with Panko breadcrumbs mixed with paprika and onion powder.

3. Dip each cheese curd into the flour, then the beaten eggs, and finally coat with the seasoned Panko breadcrumbs, pressing gently to adhere.

4. Place the breaded cheese curds in a single layer in the air fryer basket.

5. Spray the cheese curds with cooking spray.

6. Air fry for 6-8 minutes, or until golden brown and crispy, shaking the basket halfway through.

7. Serve hot with marinara sauce for dipping.

Nutritional Info: Calories: 200 | Fat: 7g | Carbs: 25g | Protein: 9g

Instant Pot Duo Crisp Air Fryer Functions Used: Air Fryer

BREAKFASTS

1. FLUFFY AIR FRIED PANCAKES

Prep: 10 mins | Cook: 10 mins | Serves: 4

Ingredients:

- 1 cup all-purpose flour (UK: 120g)

- 2 tablespoons granulated sugar (UK: 25g)

- 2 teaspoons baking powder (UK: 10g)

- 1/2 teaspoon salt (UK: 2.5g)

- 1 cup milk (UK: 240ml)

- 2 tablespoons unsalted butter, melted (UK: 30g)

- 1 large egg

- Cooking spray or melted butter, for greasing

Instructions:

1. Preheat the Instant Pot Duo Crisp Air Fryer to 350°F (175°C).

2. In a large bowl, whisk together the flour, sugar, baking powder, and salt.

3. In another bowl, whisk together the milk, melted butter, and egg.

4. Pour the wet ingredients into the dry ingredients and stir until just combined.

5. Lightly grease the air fryer basket with cooking spray or melted butter.

6. Spoon about 1/4 cup of batter onto the greased basket, leaving space between each pancake.

7. Air fry for 5 minutes, then flip the pancakes and air fry for an additional 3-5 minutes until golden brown and cooked through.

8. Repeat with the remaining batter.

9. Serve warm with maple syrup, fresh fruit, or your favorite toppings.

Nutritional Info: Calories: 190 | Fat: 6g | Carbs: 28g | Protein: 6g

Instant Pot Duo Crisp Air Fryer Functions Used: Air Fryer

2. CRISPY AIR FRIED WAFFLES

Prep: 15 mins | Cook: 10 mins | Serves: 4

Ingredients:

- 1 1/2 cups all-purpose flour (UK: 180g)
- 2 tablespoons granulated sugar (UK: 25g)
- 1 tablespoon baking powder (UK: 15g)
- 1/2 teaspoon salt (UK: 2.5g)
- 1 1/4 cups milk (UK: 300ml)
- 1/3 cup vegetable oil (UK: 80ml)
- 1 large egg
- Cooking spray or melted butter, for greasing

Instructions:

1. Preheat the Instant Pot Duo Crisp Air Fryer to 360°F (180°C).

2. In a large bowl, whisk together the flour, sugar, baking powder, and salt.

3. In another bowl, whisk together the milk, vegetable oil, and egg.

4. Pour the wet ingredients into the dry ingredients and stir until just combined.

5. Lightly grease the waffle iron with cooking spray or melted butter.

6. Pour enough batter onto the preheated waffle iron to cover the waffle grid.

7. Close the lid and cook for about 5-7 minutes, or until the waffles are golden brown and crisp.

8. Carefully remove the waffles from the waffle iron and repeat with the remaining batter.

9. Serve warm with your favorite toppings such as syrup, fresh fruit, or whipped cream.

Nutritional Info: Calories: 280 | Fat: 14g | Carbs: 34g | Protein: 6g

Instant Pot Duo Crisp Air Fryer Functions Used: Air Fryer (with waffle iron attachment)

3. AIR FRIED FRENCH TOAST STICKS

Prep: 10 mins | Cook: 10 mins | Serves: 4

Ingredients:

- 8 slices of bread, preferably slightly stale (UK: 8 slices of bread)

- 2 large eggs

- 1/4 cup milk (UK: 60ml)

- 1 teaspoon vanilla extract (UK: 5ml)

- 1/2 teaspoon ground cinnamon (UK: 2.5g)

- Cooking spray or melted butter, for greasing

Instructions:

1. Preheat the Instant Pot Duo Crisp Air Fryer to 360°F (180°C).

2. Cut each slice of bread into strips, about 1 inch wide.

3. In a shallow bowl, whisk together the eggs, milk, vanilla extract, and ground cinnamon.

4. Dip each bread strip into the egg mixture, coating both sides evenly.

5. Lightly grease the air fryer basket with cooking spray or melted butter.

6. Arrange the coated bread strips in a single layer in the air fryer basket, making sure they're not overcrowded.

7. Air fry at 360°F (180°C) for about 5 minutes, then flip the sticks over and continue to air fry for another 4-5 minutes, or until golden brown and crispy.

8. Repeat with any remaining bread strips.

9. Serve warm with maple syrup or your favorite dipping sauce.

Nutritional Info: Calories: 180 | Fat: 7g | Carbs: 20g | Protein: 8g

Instant Pot Duo Crisp Air Fryer Functions Used: Air Fryer

4. AIR FRIED HASH BROWNS

Prep: 10 mins | Cook: 20 mins | Serves: 4

Ingredients:

- 4 medium russet potatoes, peeled and grated (UK: 4 medium potatoes)

- 1 small onion, grated (UK: 1 small onion)

- 2 tablespoons all-purpose flour (UK: 30g)

- 1 teaspoon salt (UK: 5g)

- 1/2 teaspoon black pepper (UK: 2.5g)

- Cooking spray or oil, for greasing

Instructions:

1. Place the grated potatoes and onion in a clean kitchen towel and squeeze out as much moisture as possible.

2. Transfer the dried potatoes and onion to a mixing bowl.

3. Add the flour, salt, and black pepper to the bowl, and toss until the potatoes are evenly coated.

4. Preheat the Instant Pot Duo Crisp Air Fryer to 375°F (190°C).

5. Grease the air fryer basket with cooking spray or oil.

6. Spoon the potato mixture into the air fryer basket, pressing down gently to form an even layer.

7. Air fry at 375°F (190°C) for 10 minutes.

8. Carefully flip the hash browns using a spatula, and air fry for an additional 8-10 minutes, or until crispy and golden brown on both sides.

9. Serve hot as a side dish or breakfast accompaniment.

Nutritional Info: Calories: 120 | Fat: 0.5g | Carbs: 26g | Protein: 3g

Instant Pot Duo Crisp Air Fryer Functions Used: Air Fryer

5. AIR FRIED BREAKFAST POTATOES

Prep: 15 mins | Cook: 20 mins | Serves: 4

Ingredients:

- 4 medium potatoes, diced (UK: 4 medium potatoes)

- 1 onion, diced (UK: 1 onion)

- 2 cloves garlic, minced (UK: 2 cloves garlic)

- 2 tablespoons olive oil (UK: 30ml)

- 1 teaspoon paprika (UK: 5g)

- 1/2 teaspoon garlic powder (UK: 2.5g)

- Salt and pepper, to taste

Instructions:

1. In a large bowl, combine the diced potatoes, onion, minced garlic, olive oil, paprika, garlic powder, salt, and pepper.

2. Toss until the potatoes are evenly coated with the seasonings.

3. Preheat the Instant Pot Duo Crisp Air Fryer to 400°F (200°C).

4. Transfer the seasoned potatoes to the air fryer basket.

5. Air fry at 400°F (200°C) for 10 minutes.

6. Shake the basket halfway through cooking to ensure even browning.

7. Continue air frying for an additional 10 minutes, or until the potatoes are crispy and golden brown.

8. Serve hot as a delicious side dish or breakfast option.

Nutritional Info: Calories: 180 | Fat: 5g | Carbs: 30g | Protein: 3g

Instant Pot Duo Crisp Air Fryer Functions Used: Air Fryer

6. AIR FRIED BACON

Prep: 5 mins | Cook: 10 mins | Serves: 4

Ingredients:

- 8 slices bacon (UK: 8 slices bacon)

Instructions:

1. Preheat the Instant Pot Duo Crisp Air Fryer to 400°F (200°C).

2. Arrange the bacon slices in a single layer in the air fryer basket, ensuring they don't overlap.

3. Air fry at 400°F (200°C) for 8-10 minutes, depending on desired crispiness.

4. Check halfway through cooking and flip the bacon slices if necessary.

5. Once done, remove the bacon from the air fryer and place it on a paper towel-lined plate to drain excess grease.

6. Serve hot as a tasty breakfast accompaniment or in sandwiches and salads.

Nutritional Info: Calories: 70 | Fat: 5g | Carbs: 0g | Protein: 6g

Instant Pot Duo Crisp Air Fryer Functions Used: Air Fryer

7. AIR FRIED SAUSAGES

Prep: 5 mins | Cook: 15 mins | Serves: 4

Ingredients:

- 8 sausages (UK: 8 sausages)

Instructions:

1. Preheat the Instant Pot Duo Crisp Air Fryer to 375°F (190°C).

2. Place the sausages in the air fryer basket, ensuring they are not overcrowded.

3. Air fry at 375°F (190°C) for 12-15 minutes, turning them halfway through cooking for even browning.

4. Check for doneness by slicing into one sausage to ensure it's cooked through.

5. Once done, remove the sausages from the air fryer and let them rest for a few minutes.

6. Serve hot with your favorite breakfast sides or in sandwiches.

Nutritional Info: Calories: 250 | Fat: 20g | Carbs: 2g | Protein: 14g

Instant Pot Duo Crisp Air Fryer Functions Used: Air Fryer

Sure, here are four more recipes for the Instant Pot Duo Crisp Air Fryer Cookbook:

8. AIR FRIED BREAKFAST BURRITOS

Prep: 15 mins | Cook: 10 mins | Serves: 4

Ingredients:

- 4 large flour tortillas (UK: 4 large flour tortillas)
- 8 large eggs (UK: 8 large eggs)
- 1 cup shredded cheddar cheese (UK: 100g shredded cheddar cheese)
- 1 cup cooked breakfast sausage (UK: 100g cooked breakfast sausage)
- 1/2 cup diced bell peppers (UK: 50g diced bell peppers)
- 1/4 cup diced onions (UK: 25g diced onions)
- Salt and pepper to taste

Instructions:

1. Preheat the Instant Pot Duo Crisp Air Fryer to 350°F (175°C).
2. In a bowl, whisk together the eggs, salt, and pepper.
3. Divide the egg mixture, cheese, sausage, bell peppers, and onions evenly among the tortillas.
4. Roll up each tortilla tightly, folding in the sides as you go.
5. Place the burritos seam side down in the air fryer basket.
6. Air fry at 350°F (175°C) for 8-10 minutes until the tortillas are crispy and golden brown.
7. Serve hot with salsa, sour cream, or your favorite toppings.

Nutritional Info: Calories: 380 | Fat: 22g | Carbs: 22g | Protein: 24g

Instant Pot Duo Crisp Air Fryer Functions Used: Air Fryer

9. AIR FRIED BREAKFAST SANDWICHES

Prep: 10 mins | Cook: 8 mins | Serves: 2

Ingredients:

- 4 slices of bread (UK: 4 slices of bread)
- 4 large eggs (UK: 4 large eggs)
- 2 slices of cheese (UK: 2 slices of cheese)
- 4 slices of cooked bacon (UK: 4 slices of cooked bacon)
- Salt and pepper to taste

Instructions:

1. Preheat the Instant Pot Duo Crisp Air Fryer to 350°F (175°C).
2. Using a cookie cutter, cut a hole in the center of each slice of bread.
3. Place the bread slices in the air fryer basket.
4. Crack an egg into each hole in the bread.

5. Season with salt and pepper.

6. Air fry at 350°F (175°C) for 6-8 minutes until the egg whites are set.

7. Top each egg with a slice of cheese and a slice of bacon.

8. Assemble the sandwiches and serve hot.

Nutritional Info: Calories: 400 | Fat: 22g | Carbs: 28g | Protein: 22g

Instant Pot Duo Crisp Air Fryer Functions Used: Air Fryer

10. AIR FRIED OMELETS

Prep: 10 mins | Cook: 10 mins | Serves: 2

Ingredients:

- 4 large eggs (UK: 4 large eggs)

- 1/4 cup diced bell peppers (UK: 25g diced bell peppers)

- 1/4 cup diced onions (UK: 25g diced onions)

- 1/4 cup diced tomatoes (UK: 25g diced tomatoes)

- 1/2 cup shredded cheddar cheese (UK: 50g shredded cheddar cheese)

- Salt and pepper to taste

Instructions:

1. Preheat the Instant Pot Duo Crisp Air Fryer to 350°F (175°C).

2. In a bowl, whisk together the eggs, salt, and pepper.

3. Divide the egg mixture evenly into two silicone muffin cups.

4. Add diced bell peppers, onions, tomatoes, and shredded cheese to each cup.

5. Place the muffin cups in the air fryer basket.

6. Air fry at 350°F (175°C) for 8-10 minutes until the omelets are set.

7. Carefully remove the omelets from the muffin cups and serve hot.

Nutritional Info: Calories: 240 | Fat: 16g | Carbs: 4g | Protein: 18g

Instant Pot Duo Crisp Air Fryer Functions Used: Air Fryer

11. AIR FRIED FRITTATAS

Prep: 15 mins | Cook: 20 mins | Serves: 4

Ingredients:

- 8 large eggs (UK: 8 large eggs)

- 1/2 cup milk (UK: 120ml milk)

- 1/2 cup diced bell peppers (UK: 50g diced bell peppers)

- 1/2 cup diced onions (UK: 50g diced onions)
- 1/2 cup diced ham (UK: 50g diced ham)
- 1/2 cup shredded cheddar cheese (UK: 50g shredded cheddar cheese)
- Salt and pepper to taste

Instructions:

1. Preheat the Instant Pot Duo Crisp Air Fryer to 350°F (175°C).

2. In a bowl, whisk together the eggs, milk, salt, and pepper.

3. Stir in diced bell peppers, onions, ham, and shredded cheese.

4. Pour the mixture into a greased cake pan that fits inside the air fryer basket.

5. Air fry at 350°F (175°C) for 18-20 minutes until the frittata is set in the middle.

6. Let it cool for a few minutes before slicing and serving.

Nutritional Info: Calories: 280 | Fat: 18g | Carbs: 6g | Protein: 22g

Instant Pot Duo Crisp Air Fryer Functions Used: Air Fryer

Certainly! Here are four more recipes for the Instant Pot Duo Crisp Air Fryer Cookbook:

12. AIR FRIED QUICHE

Prep: 15 mins | Cook: 25 mins | Serves: 6

Ingredients:

- 1 ready-made pie crust (UK: 1 ready-made pie crust)
- 6 large eggs (UK: 6 large eggs)
- 1/2 cup milk (UK: 120ml milk)
- 1 cup chopped spinach (UK: 100g chopped spinach)
- 1/2 cup diced ham (UK: 50g diced ham)
- 1/2 cup shredded cheddar cheese (UK: 50g shredded cheddar cheese)
- Salt and pepper to taste

Instructions:

1. Preheat the Instant Pot Duo Crisp Air Fryer to 350°F (175°C).

2. Line a pie dish with the ready-made pie crust.

3. In a bowl, whisk together the eggs, milk, salt, and pepper.

4. Stir in chopped spinach, diced ham, and shredded cheese.

5. Pour the mixture into the pie crust.

6. Place the pie dish in the air fryer basket.

7. Air fry at 350°F (175°C) for 20-25 minutes until the quiche is set and golden brown.

8. Let it cool for a few minutes before slicing and serving.

Nutritional Info: Calories: 280 | Fat: 18g | Carbs: 15g | Protein: 16g

Instant Pot Duo Crisp Air Fryer Functions Used: Air Fryer

13. AIR FRIED CINNAMON ROLLS

Prep: 15 mins | Cook: 10 mins | Serves: 4

Ingredients:

- 1 can refrigerated cinnamon rolls with icing (UK: 1 can refrigerated cinnamon rolls with icing)

- Cooking spray (UK: Cooking spray)

Instructions:

1. Preheat the Instant Pot Duo Crisp Air Fryer to 350°F (175°C).

2. Spray the air fryer basket with cooking spray.

3. Place the cinnamon rolls in the air fryer basket, leaving space between each roll.

4. Air fry at 350°F (175°C) for 8-10 minutes until the rolls are golden brown and cooked through.

5. Remove from the air fryer and let them cool for a few minutes.

6. Drizzle with the included icing before serving.

Nutritional Info: Calories: 320 | Fat: 10g | Carbs: 52g | Protein: 4g

Instant Pot Duo Crisp Air Fryer Functions Used: Air Fryer

14. AIR FRIED DONUTS

Prep: 20 mins | Cook: 10 mins | Serves: 6

Ingredients:

- 1 can refrigerated biscuits (UK: 1 can refrigerated biscuits)

- 1/2 cup powdered sugar (UK: 50g powdered sugar)

- 2 tablespoons milk (UK: 30ml milk)

- 1/2 teaspoon vanilla extract (UK: 2.5ml vanilla extract)

- Cooking spray (UK: Cooking spray)

Instructions:

1. Preheat the Instant Pot Duo Crisp Air Fryer to 350°F (175°C).

2. Spray the air fryer basket with cooking spray.

3. Cut a hole in the center of each biscuit to form a donut shape.

4. Place the donuts in the air fryer basket, leaving space between each one.

5. Air fry at 350°F (175°C) for 8-10 minutes until the donuts are golden brown and cooked through.

6. In a bowl, whisk together the powdered sugar, milk, and vanilla extract to make the glaze.

7. Dip each donut into the glaze, coating it evenly.

8. Let them cool for a few minutes before serving.

Nutritional Info: Calories: 220 | Fat: 7g | Carbs: 36g | Protein: 4g

Instant Pot Duo Crisp Air Fryer Functions Used: Air Fryer

15. AIR FRIED GRANOLA

Prep: 5 mins | Cook: 15 mins | Serves: 6

Ingredients:

- 2 cups old-fashioned oats (UK: 200g old-fashioned oats)
- 1/2 cup chopped nuts (such as almonds or walnuts) (UK: 50g chopped nuts)
- 1/4 cup honey (UK: 60ml honey)
- 2 tablespoons melted coconut oil (UK: 30ml melted coconut oil)
- 1 teaspoon vanilla extract (UK: 5ml vanilla extract)
- 1/2 teaspoon ground cinnamon (UK: 2.5ml ground cinnamon)
- Pinch of salt

Instructions:

1. In a bowl, combine the oats, chopped nuts, honey, melted coconut oil, vanilla extract, ground cinnamon, and a pinch of salt.

2. Spread the mixture evenly in the air fryer basket.

3. Air fry at 300°F (150°C) for 15 minutes, stirring halfway through, until the granola is golden brown and crispy.

4. Let it cool completely before serving or storing in an airtight container.

Nutritional Info: Calories: 220 | Fat: 10g | Carbs: 28g | Protein: 5g

Instant Pot Duo Crisp Air Fryer Functions Used: Air Fryer

CHICKEN MAIN DISHES

1. AIR FRIED CHICKEN TENDERS

Prep: 15 mins | Cook: 12 mins | Serves: 4

Ingredients:

- 1 lb chicken tenders (UK: 450g chicken tenders)

- 1 cup breadcrumbs (UK: 100g breadcrumbs)
- 1/2 cup grated Parmesan cheese (UK: 50g grated Parmesan cheese)
- 1 teaspoon garlic powder (UK: 5ml garlic powder)
- 1 teaspoon paprika (UK: 5ml paprika)
- Salt and pepper to taste
- Cooking spray (UK: Cooking spray)

Instructions:

1. Preheat the Instant Pot Duo Crisp Air Fryer to 400°F (200°C).
2. In a shallow dish, mix breadcrumbs, Parmesan cheese, garlic powder, paprika, salt, and pepper.
3. Dip each chicken tender into the breadcrumb mixture, ensuring they are evenly coated.
4. Spray the air fryer basket with cooking spray.
5. Place the chicken tenders in the basket, leaving space between each one.
6. Air fry at 400°F (200°C) for 10-12 minutes, flipping halfway through, until golden brown and cooked through.
7. Serve hot with your favorite dipping sauce.

Nutritional Info: Calories: 280 | Fat: 8g | Carbs: 18g | Protein: 30g

Instant Pot Duo Crisp Air Fryer Functions Used: Air Fryer

2. AIR FRIED CHICKEN WINGS

Prep: 10 mins | Cook: 25 mins | Serves: 4

Ingredients:

- 2 lbs chicken wings (UK: 900g chicken wings)
- 2 tablespoons olive oil (UK: 30ml olive oil)
- 1 teaspoon garlic powder (UK: 5ml garlic powder)
- 1 teaspoon onion powder (UK: 5ml onion powder)
- Salt and pepper to taste
- 1/2 cup buffalo sauce (UK: 120ml buffalo sauce)

Instructions:

1. In a large bowl, toss chicken wings with olive oil, garlic powder, onion powder, salt, and pepper until evenly coated.
2. Preheat the Instant Pot Duo Crisp Air Fryer to 380°F (190°C).
3. Place the chicken wings in the air fryer basket, making sure they are not overcrowded.
4. Air fry at 380°F (190°C) for 20-25 minutes, flipping halfway through, until crispy and cooked through.
5. In a separate bowl, toss the cooked wings with buffalo sauce until coated.

6. Serve hot with celery sticks and ranch or blue cheese dressing.

Nutritional Info: Calories: 320 | Fat: 22g | Carbs: 2g | Protein: 28g

Instant Pot Duo Crisp Air Fryer Functions Used: Air Fryer

3. AIR FRIED CHICKEN DRUMSTICKS

Prep: 10 mins | Cook: 30 mins | Serves: 4

Ingredients:

- 8 chicken drumsticks (UK: 8 chicken drumsticks)

- 2 tablespoons olive oil (UK: 30ml olive oil)

- 1 teaspoon smoked paprika (UK: 5ml smoked paprika)

- 1 teaspoon dried thyme (UK: 5ml dried thyme)

- Salt and pepper to taste

Instructions:

1. In a large bowl, toss chicken drumsticks with olive oil, smoked paprika, dried thyme, salt, and pepper until well coated.

2. Preheat the Instant Pot Duo Crisp Air Fryer to 380°F (190°C).

3. Place the chicken drumsticks in the air fryer basket, making sure they are not touching.

4. Air fry at 380°F (190°C) for 25-30 minutes, flipping halfway through, until golden brown and cooked through.

5. Serve hot with your favorite dipping sauce or side dishes.

Nutritional Info: Calories: 250 | Fat: 14g | Carbs: 0g | Protein: 30g

Instant Pot Duo Crisp Air Fryer Functions Used: Air Fryer

4. AIR FRIED CHICKEN THIGHS

Prep: 10 mins | Cook: 25 mins | Serves: 4

Ingredients:

- 4 bone-in, skin-on chicken thighs (UK: 4 bone-in, skin-on chicken thighs)

- 2 tablespoons soy sauce (UK: 30ml soy sauce)

- 1 tablespoon honey (UK: 15ml honey)

- 1 teaspoon garlic powder (UK: 5ml garlic powder)

- 1 teaspoon smoked paprika (UK: 5ml smoked paprika)

- Salt and pepper to taste

Instructions:

1. In a bowl, whisk together soy sauce, honey, garlic powder, smoked paprika, salt, and pepper.

2. Marinate the chicken thighs in the sauce for at least 30 minutes or overnight in the refrigerator.

3. Preheat the Instant Pot Duo Crisp Air Fryer to 380°F (190°C).

4. Remove the chicken thighs from the marinade and pat them dry with paper towels.

5. Place the chicken thighs in the air fryer basket, skin side down.

6. Air fry at 380°F (190°C) for 12 minutes, then flip and cook for another 10-12 minutes until the skin is crispy and the chicken is cooked through.

7. Serve hot with your favorite side dishes.

Nutritional Info: Calories: 320 | Fat: 18g | Carbs: 5g | Protein: 30g

Instant Pot Duo Crisp Air Fryer Functions Used: Air Fryer

5. AIR FRIED CHICKEN BREASTS

Prep: 10 mins | Cook: 20 mins | Serves: 4

Ingredients:

- 4 boneless, skinless chicken breasts (UK: 4 boneless, skinless chicken breasts)

- 1/4 cup all-purpose flour (UK: 30g all-purpose flour)

- 1 teaspoon garlic powder (UK: 5ml garlic powder)

- 1 teaspoon onion powder (UK: 5ml onion powder)

- 1 teaspoon paprika (UK: 5ml paprika)

- Salt and pepper to taste

- Cooking spray (UK: Cooking spray)

Instructions:

1. Preheat the Instant Pot Duo Crisp Air Fryer to 375°F (190°C).

2. In a shallow dish, mix flour, garlic powder, onion powder, paprika, salt, and pepper.

3. Dredge each chicken breast in the flour mixture, shaking off any excess.

4. Spray the air fryer basket with cooking spray.

5. Place the chicken breasts in the basket, ensuring they are not touching.

6. Air fry at 375°F (190°C) for 18-20 minutes, flipping halfway through, until golden brown and cooked through.

7. Serve hot with your favorite side dishes.

Nutritional Info: Calories: 220 | Fat: 3g | Carbs: 10g | Protein: 35g

Instant Pot Duo Crisp Air Fryer Functions Used: Air Fryer

6. AIR FRIED CHICKEN PARMESAN

Prep: 15 mins | Cook: 25 mins | Serves: 4

Ingredients:

- 4 boneless, skinless chicken breasts (UK: 4 boneless, skinless chicken breasts)

- 1 cup breadcrumbs (UK: 100g breadcrumbs)

- 1/2 cup grated Parmesan cheese (UK: 50g grated Parmesan cheese)

- 1 teaspoon Italian seasoning (UK: 5ml Italian seasoning)

- 1 cup marinara sauce (UK: 240ml marinara sauce)

- 1 cup shredded mozzarella cheese (UK: 100g shredded mozzarella cheese)

- Cooking spray (UK: Cooking spray)

Instructions:

1. Preheat the Instant Pot Duo Crisp Air Fryer to 375°F (190°C).

2. In a shallow dish, mix breadcrumbs, Parmesan cheese, and Italian seasoning.

3. Dredge each chicken breast in the breadcrumb mixture, pressing gently to adhere.

4. Spray the air fryer basket with cooking spray.

5. Place the chicken breasts in the basket and air fry at 375°F (190°C) for 20 minutes.

6. Remove the chicken breasts from the air fryer and top each with marinara sauce and shredded mozzarella cheese.

7. Return the chicken breasts to the air fryer and air fry for an additional 5 minutes, or until the cheese is melted and bubbly.

8. Serve hot with pasta or a side salad.

Nutritional Info: Calories: 350 | Fat: 12g | Carbs: 20g | Protein: 40g

Instant Pot Duo Crisp Air Fryer Functions Used: Air Fryer

7. AIR FRIED BUFFALO CHICKEN

Prep: 15 mins | Cook: 20 mins | Serves: 4

Ingredients:

- 4 boneless, skinless chicken breasts (UK: 4 boneless, skinless chicken breasts)

- 1/2 cup buffalo sauce (UK: 120ml buffalo sauce)

- 2 tablespoons melted butter (UK: 30ml melted butter)

- 1 teaspoon garlic powder (UK: 5ml garlic powder)

- Salt and pepper to taste

- Ranch or blue cheese dressing for serving (UK: Ranch or blue cheese dressing for serving)

Instructions:

1. In a bowl, whisk together buffalo sauce, melted butter, garlic powder, salt, and pepper.

2. Add the chicken breasts to the bowl and toss until evenly coated.

3. Preheat the Instant Pot Duo Crisp Air Fryer to 375°F (190°C).

4. Place the chicken breasts in the air fryer basket and air fry at 375°F (190°C) for 18-20 minutes, flipping halfway through, until cooked through.

5. Serve hot with ranch or blue cheese dressing and celery sticks.

Nutritional Info: Calories: 280 | Fat: 10g | Carbs: 2g | Protein: 40g

Instant Pot Duo Crisp Air Fryer Functions Used: Air Fryer

8. AIR FRIED FRIED CHICKEN

Prep: 20 mins | Cook: 30 mins | Serves: 4

Ingredients:

- 8 chicken drumsticks (UK: 8 chicken drumsticks)

- 1 cup buttermilk (UK: 240ml buttermilk)

- 1 cup all-purpose flour (UK: 120g all-purpose flour)

- 1 teaspoon garlic powder (UK: 5ml garlic powder)

- 1 teaspoon paprika (UK: 5ml paprika)

- Salt and pepper to taste

- Cooking spray (UK: Cooking spray)

Instructions:

1. In a bowl, marinate chicken drumsticks in buttermilk for at least 1 hour or overnight in the refrigerator.

2. In a shallow dish, mix flour, garlic powder, paprika, salt, and pepper.

3. Dredge each chicken drumstick in the flour mixture, shaking off any excess.

4. Preheat the Instant Pot Duo Crisp Air Fryer to 375°F (190°C).

5. Spray the air fryer basket with cooking spray.

6. Place the chicken drumsticks in the basket and air fry at 375°F (190°C) for 25-30 minutes, flipping halfway through, until golden brown and cooked through.

7. Serve hot with your favorite dipping sauce.

Nutritional Info: Calories: 320 | Fat: 12g | Carbs: 20g | Protein: 30g

Instant Pot Duo Crisp Air Fryer Functions Used: Air Fryer

Certainly! Here are four more recipes for chicken main dishes using the Instant Pot Duo Crisp Air Fryer:

9. AIR FRIED CHICKEN FAJITAS

Prep: 15 mins | Cook: 20 mins | Serves: 4

Ingredients:

- 1 lb boneless, skinless chicken breasts, sliced (UK: 450g boneless, skinless chicken breasts, sliced)

- 2 bell peppers, sliced (UK: 2 bell peppers, sliced)

- 1 onion, sliced (UK: 1 onion, sliced)

- 2 tablespoons fajita seasoning (UK: 30ml fajita seasoning)

- 2 tablespoons olive oil (UK: 30ml olive oil)

- Salt and pepper to taste

- 8 small flour tortillas, warmed (UK: 8 small flour tortillas, warmed)

- Optional toppings: salsa, sour cream, guacamole, shredded cheese

Instructions:

1. In a bowl, toss chicken slices, bell peppers, and onions with fajita seasoning, olive oil, salt, and pepper until evenly coated.

2. Preheat the Instant Pot Duo Crisp Air Fryer to 375°F (190°C).

3. Place the chicken mixture in the air fryer basket and air fry at 375°F (190°C) for 18-20 minutes, stirring halfway through, until chicken is cooked through and vegetables are tender.

4. Serve the chicken fajita mixture in warmed tortillas with desired toppings.

Nutritional Info: Calories: 350 | Fat: 12g | Carbs: 30g | Protein: 25g

Instant Pot Duo Crisp Air Fryer Functions Used: Air Fryer

10. AIR FRIED CHICKEN TACOS

Prep: 15 mins | Cook: 20 mins | Serves: 4

Ingredients:

- 1 lb boneless, skinless chicken thighs, diced (UK: 450g boneless, skinless chicken thighs, diced)

- 2 tablespoons taco seasoning (UK: 30ml taco seasoning)

- 1 tablespoon olive oil (UK: 15ml olive oil)

- Salt and pepper to taste

- 8 small corn tortillas, warmed (UK: 8 small corn tortillas, warmed)

- Optional toppings: shredded lettuce, diced tomatoes, shredded cheese, salsa, sour cream

Instructions:

1. In a bowl, toss diced chicken thighs with taco seasoning, olive oil, salt, and pepper until evenly coated.

2. Preheat the Instant Pot Duo Crisp Air Fryer to 375°F (190°C).

3. Place the seasoned chicken thighs in the air fryer basket and air fry at 375°F (190°C) for 18-20 minutes, stirring halfway through, until chicken is cooked through and slightly crispy.

4. Serve the chicken taco filling in warmed corn tortillas with desired toppings.

Nutritional Info: Calories: 300 | Fat: 10g | Carbs: 20g | Protein: 25g

Instant Pot Duo Crisp Air Fryer Functions Used: Air Fryer

11. AIR FRIED CHICKEN ENCHILADAS

Prep: 20 mins | Cook: 25 mins | Serves: 4

Ingredients:

- 1 lb cooked shredded chicken (UK: 450g cooked shredded chicken)

- 1 cup enchilada sauce (UK: 240ml enchilada sauce)

- 8 small flour tortillas (UK: 8 small flour tortillas)

- 1 cup shredded cheese (UK: 100g shredded cheese)

- Optional toppings: diced onions, chopped cilantro, sour cream, avocado slices

Instructions:

1. Preheat the Instant Pot Duo Crisp Air Fryer to 375°F (190°C).

2. Spread a spoonful of enchilada sauce onto each tortilla.

3. Divide the shredded chicken evenly among the tortillas.

4. Roll up the tortillas and place seam-side down in the air fryer basket.

5. Pour the remaining enchilada sauce over the rolled tortillas and sprinkle with shredded cheese.

6. Air fry at 375°F (190°C) for 20-25 minutes, until the cheese is melted and bubbly.

7. Serve hot with optional toppings.

Nutritional Info: Calories: 380 | Fat: 15g | Carbs: 30g | Protein: 30g

Instant Pot Duo Crisp Air Fryer Functions Used: Air Fryer

12. AIR FRIED CHICKEN POT PIE

Prep: 30 mins | Cook: 30 mins | Serves: 4

Ingredients:

- 1 lb cooked shredded chicken (UK: 450g cooked shredded chicken)

- 1 cup mixed vegetables (UK: 100g mixed vegetables)

- 1 cup chicken broth (UK: 240ml chicken broth)

- 1/2 cup milk (UK: 120ml milk)

- 3 tablespoons all-purpose flour (UK: 30g all-purpose flour)

- 1 teaspoon garlic powder (UK: 5ml garlic powder)

- Salt and pepper to taste

- 1 sheet puff pastry, thawed (UK: 1 sheet puff pastry, thawed)

- 1 egg, beaten (UK: 1 egg, beaten)

Instructions:

1. In a saucepan, combine chicken, mixed vegetables, chicken broth, milk, flour, garlic powder, salt, and pepper.

2. Cook over medium heat until the mixture thickens, stirring frequently.

3. Preheat the Instant Pot Duo Crisp Air Fryer to 375°F (190°C).

4. Pour the chicken mixture into a baking dish.

5. Roll out the puff pastry sheet and place it over the baking dish, trimming any excess.

6. Brush the pastry with beaten egg.

7. Air fry at 375°F (190°C) for 25-30 minutes, until the pastry is golden brown and the filling is bubbly.

8. Serve hot.

Nutritional Info: Calories: 420 | Fat: 20g | Carbs: 35g | Protein: 25g

Instant Pot Duo Crisp Air Fryer Functions Used: Air Fryer

13. AIR FRIED CHICKEN MARSALA

Prep: 15 mins | Cook: 25 mins | Serves: 4

Ingredients:

- 4 boneless, skinless chicken breasts (UK: 4 boneless, skinless chicken breasts)

- Salt and pepper to taste

- 1/2 cup all-purpose flour (UK: 60g all-purpose flour)

- 4 tablespoons olive oil (UK: 60ml olive oil)

- 2 cups sliced mushrooms (UK: 200g sliced mushrooms)

- 1/2 cup Marsala wine (UK: 120ml Marsala wine)

- 1/2 cup chicken broth (UK: 120ml chicken broth)

- 1/4 cup heavy cream (UK: 60ml heavy cream)

- 2 tablespoons chopped fresh parsley (UK: 30ml chopped fresh parsley)

Instructions:

1. Season chicken breasts with salt and pepper. Dredge each breast in flour, shaking off any excess.

2. Preheat the Instant Pot Duo Crisp Air Fryer to 375°F (190°C).

3. Add 2 tablespoons of olive oil to the air fryer basket. Place chicken breasts in the basket and air fry for 8-10 minutes, flipping halfway through, until golden brown and cooked through. Remove and set aside.

4. Add the remaining olive oil to the air fryer basket along with sliced mushrooms. Air fry for 5-7 minutes, until mushrooms are tender.

5. Deglaze the basket with Marsala wine, scraping up any browned bits from the bottom. Cook for 2-3 minutes to reduce slightly.

6. Stir in chicken broth and heavy cream. Cook for another 2-3 minutes, until the sauce thickens.

7. Return chicken breasts to the air fryer basket, spooning the mushroom sauce over them.

8. Air fry for an additional 5 minutes, until the sauce is bubbly.

9. Garnish with chopped parsley before serving.

Nutritional Info: Calories: 380 | Fat: 18g | Carbs: 15g | Protein: 35g

Instant Pot Duo Crisp Air Fryer Functions Used: Air Fryer

14. AIR FRIED CHICKEN CORDON BLEU

Prep: 20 mins | Cook: 25 mins | Serves: 4

Ingredients:

- 4 boneless, skinless chicken breasts (UK: 4 boneless, skinless chicken breasts)

- Salt and pepper to taste

- 4 slices ham (UK: 4 slices ham)

- 4 slices Swiss cheese (UK: 4 slices Swiss cheese)

- 1/2 cup all-purpose flour (UK: 60g all-purpose flour)

- 2 eggs, beaten (UK: 2 eggs, beaten)

- 1 cup breadcrumbs (UK: 100g breadcrumbs)

- 2 tablespoons olive oil (UK: 30ml olive oil)

Instructions:

1. Season chicken breasts with salt and pepper. Make a slit in the side of each breast to form a pocket.

2. Place a slice of ham and a slice of Swiss cheese inside each pocket.

3. Dredge each stuffed chicken breast in flour, shaking off any excess. Dip in beaten eggs, then coat with breadcrumbs.

4. Preheat the Instant Pot Duo Crisp Air Fryer to 375°F (190°C).

5. Brush the air fryer basket with olive oil. Place the stuffed chicken breasts in the basket.

6. Air fry for 20-25 minutes, flipping halfway through, until chicken is golden brown and cooked through.

7. Serve hot.

Nutritional Info: Calories: 420 | Fat: 20g | Carbs: 20g | Protein: 35g

Instant Pot Duo Crisp Air Fryer Functions Used: Air Fryer

15. AIR FRIED CHICKEN PICCATA

Prep: 15 mins | Cook: 20 mins | Serves: 4

Ingredients:

- 4 boneless, skinless chicken breasts (UK: 4 boneless, skinless chicken breasts)

- Salt and pepper to taste

- 1/2 cup all-purpose flour (UK: 60g all-purpose flour)

- 4 tablespoons unsalted butter (UK: 60g unsalted butter)

- 1/4 cup fresh lemon juice (UK: 60ml fresh lemon juice)

- 1/2 cup chicken broth (UK: 120ml chicken broth)

- 1/4 cup capers, drained (UK: 30g capers, drained)

- 2 tablespoons chopped fresh parsley (UK: 30ml chopped fresh parsley)

Instructions:

1. Season chicken breasts with salt and pepper. Dredge each breast in flour, shaking off any excess.

2. Preheat the Instant Pot Duo Crisp Air Fryer to 375°F (190°C).

3. Add 2 tablespoons of butter to the air fryer basket. Place chicken breasts in the basket and air fry for 8-10 minutes, flipping halfway through, until golden brown and cooked through. Remove and set aside.

4. Add the remaining butter to the air fryer basket along with fresh lemon juice, chicken broth, and capers. Cook for 2-3 minutes, stirring occasionally, until the sauce thickens slightly.

5. Return chicken breasts to the air fryer basket, spooning the lemon caper sauce over them.

6. Air fry for an additional 5 minutes, until the sauce is heated through.

7. Garnish with chopped parsley before serving.

Nutritional Info: Calories: 350 | Fat: 15g | Carbs: 15g | Protein: 35g

Instant Pot Duo Crisp Air Fryer Functions Used: Air Fryer

BEEF MAIN DISHES

1. AIR FRIED BEEF JERKY

Prep: 10 mins | Cook: 4 hours | Serves: 8

Ingredients:

- 2 pounds beef top round, thinly sliced (UK: 900g beef top round, thinly sliced)

- 1/2 cup soy sauce (UK: 120ml soy sauce)

- 1/4 cup Worcestershire sauce (UK: 60ml Worcestershire sauce)

- 2 tablespoons brown sugar (UK: 25g brown sugar)

- 1 teaspoon garlic powder (UK: 1 teaspoon garlic powder)

- 1 teaspoon onion powder (UK: 1 teaspoon onion powder)

- 1 teaspoon black pepper (UK: 1 teaspoon black pepper)

Instructions:

1. In a bowl, combine soy sauce, Worcestershire sauce, brown sugar, garlic powder, onion powder, and black pepper to make the marinade.

2. Place thinly sliced beef in a resealable plastic bag or a shallow dish. Pour the marinade over the beef, ensuring all slices are coated. Marinate in the refrigerator for at least 4 hours or overnight.

3. Preheat the Instant Pot Duo Crisp Air Fryer to 160°F (70°C) using the dehydrate function.

4. Remove beef slices from the marinade and pat dry with paper towels.

5. Arrange the beef slices on the air fryer trays in a single layer, leaving space between each slice for air circulation.

6. Dehydrate the beef slices for 4 hours, flipping halfway through, until they are dry and chewy.

7. Allow the beef jerky to cool completely before storing in an airtight container.

Nutritional Info: Calories: 150 | Fat: 4g | Carbs: 3g | Protein: 25g

Instant Pot Duo Crisp Air Fryer Functions Used: Dehydrate

2. AIR FRIED STEAK BITES

Prep: 15 mins | Cook: 10 mins | Serves: 4

Ingredients:

- 1 pound sirloin steak, cut into bite-sized pieces (UK: 450g sirloin steak, cut into bite-sized pieces)
- 2 tablespoons olive oil (UK: 30ml olive oil)
- 2 teaspoons garlic powder (UK: 2 teaspoons garlic powder)
- 1 teaspoon paprika (UK: 1 teaspoon paprika)
- Salt and pepper to taste
- Optional: chopped fresh parsley for garnish

Instructions:

1. Preheat the Instant Pot Duo Crisp Air Fryer to 400°F (200°C) using the air fry function.

2. In a bowl, toss the steak pieces with olive oil, garlic powder, paprika, salt, and pepper until evenly coated.

3. Place the seasoned steak pieces in the air fryer basket in a single layer, ensuring they are not overcrowded.

4. Air fry for 8-10 minutes, shaking the basket halfway through, until the steak reaches your desired level of doneness.

5. Transfer the steak bites to a serving plate, garnish with chopped parsley if desired, and serve hot.

Nutritional Info: Calories: 280 | Fat: 15g | Carbs: 1g | Protein: 32g

Instant Pot Duo Crisp Air Fryer Functions Used: Air Fry

3. AIR FRIED STEAK FAJITAS

Prep: 20 mins | Cook: 15 mins | Serves: 4

Ingredients:

- 1 pound flank steak, thinly sliced (UK: 450g flank steak, thinly sliced)

- 2 bell peppers, thinly sliced (UK: 2 bell peppers, thinly sliced)

- 1 onion, thinly sliced (UK: 1 onion, thinly sliced)

- 2 tablespoons olive oil (UK: 30ml olive oil)

- 2 tablespoons fajita seasoning (UK: 2 tablespoons fajita seasoning)

- Salt and pepper to taste

- Flour tortillas, for serving

- Optional toppings: salsa, guacamole, sour cream, shredded cheese

Instructions:

1. Preheat the Instant Pot Duo Crisp Air Fryer to 400°F (200°C) using the air fry function.

2. In a bowl, toss the sliced flank steak, bell peppers, and onion with olive oil and fajita seasoning until evenly coated. Season with salt and pepper.

3. Place the seasoned steak and vegetables in the air fryer basket in a single layer.

4. Air fry for 12-15 minutes, stirring halfway through, until the steak is cooked to your liking and the vegetables are tender and slightly charred.

5. Warm the flour tortillas in the air fryer for 1-2 minutes, if desired.

6. Serve the steak and vegetable mixture with warm tortillas and optional toppings, and enjoy!

Nutritional Info: Calories: 320 | Fat: 15g | Carbs: 20g | Protein: 25g

Instant Pot Duo Crisp Air Fryer Functions Used: Air Fry

4. AIR FRIED STEAK TACOS

Prep: 20 mins | Cook: 15 mins | Serves: 4

Ingredients:

- 1 pound skirt steak (UK: 450g skirt steak)

- 2 tablespoons olive oil (UK: 30ml olive oil)

- 2 teaspoons chili powder (UK: 2 teaspoons chili powder)

- 1 teaspoon cumin (UK: 1 teaspoon cumin)

- 1 teaspoon garlic powder (UK: 1 teaspoon garlic powder)

- Salt and pepper to taste

- 8 small corn or flour tortillas

- Optional toppings: diced onion, chopped cilantro, salsa, lime wedges

Instructions:

1. Preheat the Instant Pot Duo Crisp Air Fryer to 400°F (200°C) using the air fry function.

2. In a bowl, combine olive oil, chili powder, cumin, garlic powder, salt, and pepper to make the marinade.

3. Place the skirt steak in the marinade, ensuring it's evenly coated. Let it marinate for at least 15 minutes.

4. Place the marinated steak in the air fryer basket.

5. Air fry for 12-15 minutes, flipping halfway through, until the steak reaches your desired level of doneness.

6. Let the steak rest for a few minutes before slicing thinly against the grain.

7. Warm the tortillas in the air fryer for 1-2 minutes.

8. Assemble the tacos by placing sliced steak on warm tortillas and adding desired toppings.

9. Serve with lime wedges on the side and enjoy!

Nutritional Info: Calories: 350 | Fat: 15g | Carbs: 20g | Protein: 30g

Instant Pot Duo Crisp Air Fryer Functions Used: Air Fry

5. AIR FRIED STEAK AND POTATOES

Prep: 15 mins | Cook: 25 mins | Serves: 4

Ingredients:

- 1 pound sirloin steak, cut into 4 pieces (UK: 450g sirloin steak, cut into 4 pieces)
- 4 medium potatoes, washed and cubed (UK: 4 medium potatoes, washed and cubed)
- 2 tablespoons olive oil (UK: 30ml olive oil)
- 2 teaspoons steak seasoning (UK: 2 teaspoons steak seasoning)
- Salt and pepper to taste
- Optional: chopped fresh parsley for garnish

Instructions:

1. Preheat the Instant Pot Duo Crisp Air Fryer to 400°F (200°C) using the air fry function.

2. In a bowl, toss the cubed potatoes with olive oil, steak seasoning, salt, and pepper until evenly coated.

3. Place the seasoned potatoes in the air fryer basket in a single layer.

4. Air fry for 15 minutes, shaking the basket halfway through, until the potatoes are golden brown and crispy.

5. Meanwhile, season the steak pieces with salt and pepper.

6. Add the seasoned steak pieces to the air fryer basket with the potatoes.

7. Air fry for an additional 8-10 minutes for medium-rare steak or longer for desired doneness, flipping halfway through.

8. Transfer the steak and potatoes to a serving plate, garnish with chopped parsley if desired, and serve hot.

Nutritional Info: Calories: 450 | Fat: 20g | Carbs: 35g | Protein: 30g

Instant Pot Duo Crisp Air Fryer Functions Used: Air Fry

6. AIR FRIED CHEESESTEAK

Prep: 20 mins | Cook: 15 mins | Serves: 4

Ingredients:

- 1 pound ribeye steak, thinly sliced (UK: 450g ribeye steak, thinly sliced)

- 2 bell peppers, thinly sliced (UK: 2 bell peppers, thinly sliced)

- 1 onion, thinly sliced (UK: 1 onion, thinly sliced)

- 8 slices provolone cheese (UK: 8 slices provolone cheese)

- 4 hoagie rolls, split (UK: 4 hoagie rolls, split)

- 2 tablespoons olive oil (UK: 30ml olive oil)

- Salt and pepper to taste

Instructions:

1. Preheat the Instant Pot Duo Crisp Air Fryer to 400°F (200°C) using the air fry function.

2. In a skillet, heat olive oil over medium heat. Add the sliced bell peppers and onions, and cook until softened, about 5 minutes. Remove from heat and set aside.

3. Season the thinly sliced ribeye steak with salt and pepper.

4. Place the seasoned steak in the air fryer basket in a single layer.

5. Air fry for 8-10 minutes, flipping halfway through, until the steak is cooked to your liking.

6. Remove the steak from the air fryer and set aside.

7. Layer the cooked steak on top of the bell peppers and onions in the skillet.

8. Top the steak with provolone cheese slices.

9. Place the skillet in the air fryer and air fry for an additional 2-3 minutes, until the cheese is melted and bubbly.

10. Toast the hoagie rolls in the air fryer for 1-2 minutes.

11. Assemble the cheesesteak sandwiches by placing the steak, peppers, and onions on the hoagie rolls.

12. Serve hot and enjoy!

Nutritional Info: Calories: 600 | Fat: 35g | Carbs: 35g | Protein: 45g

Instant Pot Duo Crisp Air Fryer Functions Used: Air Fry

7. AIR FRIED BEEF EMPANADAS

Prep: 30 mins | Cook: 15 mins | Serves: 6

Ingredients:

- 1 pound ground beef (UK: 450g ground beef)

- 1 onion, finely chopped (UK: 1 onion, finely chopped)

- 2 cloves garlic, minced (UK: 2 cloves garlic, minced)

- 1 teaspoon ground cumin (UK: 1 teaspoon ground cumin)

- 1 teaspoon paprika (UK: 1 teaspoon paprika)

- Salt and pepper to taste

- 1/2 cup frozen peas (UK: 75g frozen peas)

- 1/2 cup frozen corn (UK: 75g frozen corn)

- 1/4 cup chopped fresh cilantro (UK: 15g chopped fresh cilantro)

- 1 package refrigerated pie crusts (2 crusts)

- 1 egg, beaten (UK: 1 egg, beaten)

Instructions:

1. Preheat the Instant Pot Duo Crisp Air Fryer to 375°F (190°C) using the air fry function.

2. In a skillet, cook the ground beef, onion, and garlic over medium heat until the beef is browned and the onion is softened.

3. Stir in the ground cumin, paprika, salt, and pepper.

4. Add the frozen peas and corn, and cook for an additional 2-3 minutes.

5. Remove from heat and stir in chopped cilantro. Let the filling cool slightly.

6. Roll out the pie crusts on a lightly floured surface and cut out circles using a round cutter or a glass.

7. Place a spoonful of the beef filling onto one half of each pie crust circle.

8. Fold the other half of the dough over the filling to form a half-moon shape. Press the edges together to seal.

9. Crimp the edges with a fork to create a decorative seal.

10. Brush the empanadas with beaten egg for a golden finish.

11. Place the empanadas in the air fryer basket in a single layer, leaving space between each one.

12. Air fry for 12-15 minutes, until the empanadas are golden brown and crispy.

13. Serve hot as a delicious snack or appetizer.

Nutritional Info: Calories: 350 | Fat: 20g | Carbs: 25g | Protein: 15g

Instant Pot Duo Crisp Air Fryer Functions Used: Air Fry

8. AIR FRIED ROAST BEEF

Prep: 15 mins | Cook: 45 mins | Serves: 6

Ingredients:

- 3 pounds beef roast (UK: 1.4kg beef roast)

- 2 tablespoons olive oil (UK: 30ml olive oil)
- 2 teaspoons garlic powder (UK: 2 teaspoons garlic powder)
- 2 teaspoons onion powder (UK: 2 teaspoons onion powder)
- 2 teaspoons dried thyme (UK: 2 teaspoons dried thyme)
- Salt and pepper to taste

Instructions:

1. Preheat the Instant Pot Duo Crisp Air Fryer to 360°F (180°C) using the roast function.

2. In a small bowl, combine olive oil, garlic powder, onion powder, dried thyme, salt, and pepper to make a seasoning paste.

3. Rub the seasoning paste all over the beef roast, ensuring it's evenly coated.

4. Place the seasoned beef roast in the air fryer basket.

5. Air fry for 45-50 minutes, flipping halfway through, until the roast reaches your desired level of doneness.

6. Remove the roast from the air fryer and let it rest for 10 minutes before slicing.

7. Slice the roast thinly against the grain and serve hot with your favorite side dishes.

Nutritional Info: Calories: 300 | Fat: 15g | Carbs: 0g | Protein: 40g

Instant Pot Duo Crisp Air Fryer Functions Used: Roast

Certainly! Here are the next four recipes for beef main dishes using the Instant Pot Duo Crisp Air Fryer:

9. AIR FRIED MEATLOAF

Prep: 15 mins | Cook: 40 mins | Serves: 6

Ingredients:

- 1 pound ground beef (UK: 450g ground beef)
- 1/2 cup breadcrumbs (UK: 60g breadcrumbs)
- 1/4 cup milk (UK: 60ml milk)
- 1/4 cup chopped onion (UK: 60g chopped onion)
- 1/4 cup chopped bell pepper (UK: 60g chopped bell pepper)
- 1 egg, beaten (UK: 1 egg, beaten)
- 2 tablespoons ketchup (UK: 30ml ketchup)
- 1 teaspoon Worcestershire sauce (UK: 1 teaspoon Worcestershire sauce)
- 1/2 teaspoon garlic powder (UK: 1/2 teaspoon garlic powder)
- Salt and pepper to taste

Instructions:

1. Preheat the Instant Pot Duo Crisp Air Fryer to 360°F (180°C) using the air fry function.

2. In a large bowl, combine ground beef, breadcrumbs, milk, chopped onion, chopped bell pepper, beaten egg, ketchup, Worcestershire sauce, garlic powder, salt, and pepper. Mix until well combined.

3. Shape the mixture into a loaf and place it in the air fryer basket.

4. Air fry for 35-40 minutes, until the meatloaf is cooked through and browned on the outside.

5. Remove the meatloaf from the air fryer and let it rest for 5-10 minutes before slicing.

6. Slice the meatloaf and serve hot with your favorite side dishes.

Nutritional Info: Calories: 300 | Fat: 15g | Carbs: 10g | Protein: 25g

Instant Pot Duo Crisp Air Fryer Functions Used: Air Fry

10. AIR FRIED BEEF WELLINGTON

Prep: 30 mins | Cook: 30 mins | Serves: 4

Ingredients:

- 1 pound beef tenderloin, trimmed (UK: 450g beef tenderloin, trimmed)

- Salt and pepper to taste

- 2 tablespoons olive oil (UK: 30ml olive oil)

- 1/2 pound mushrooms, finely chopped (UK: 225g mushrooms, finely chopped)

- 2 cloves garlic, minced (UK: 2 cloves garlic, minced)

- 2 tablespoons chopped fresh parsley (UK: 30g chopped fresh parsley)

- 4 slices prosciutto (UK: 4 slices prosciutto)

- 1 sheet puff pastry, thawed (UK: 1 sheet puff pastry, thawed)

- 1 egg, beaten (UK: 1 egg, beaten)

Instructions:

1. Preheat the Instant Pot Duo Crisp Air Fryer to 400°F (200°C) using the air fry function.

2. Season the beef tenderloin with salt and pepper.

3. Heat olive oil in a skillet over medium heat. Add the chopped mushrooms and garlic, and cook until the mushrooms release their moisture and turn golden brown.

4. Stir in the chopped parsley and cook for another minute. Remove from heat and let cool slightly.

5. Place a slice of prosciutto on a clean surface. Spread a layer of the mushroom mixture over the prosciutto.

6. Place the seasoned beef tenderloin on top of the mushroom mixture.

7. Wrap the prosciutto around the beef tenderloin, sealing it tightly.

8. Roll out the puff pastry on a lightly floured surface. Place the wrapped beef tenderloin in the center of the pastry.

9. Wrap the puff pastry around the beef tenderloin, sealing the edges. Trim any excess pastry if necessary.

10. Brush the pastry with beaten egg for a golden finish.

11. Place the beef Wellington in the air fryer basket.

12. Air fry for 25-30 minutes, until the pastry is golden brown and the beef reaches your desired level of doneness.

13. Remove from the air fryer and let it rest for 5-10 minutes before slicing.

14. Slice the beef Wellington and serve hot with your favorite side dishes.

Nutritional Info: Calories: 400 | Fat: 25g | Carbs: 20g | Protein: 25g

Instant Pot Duo Crisp Air Fryer Functions Used: Air Fry

11. AIR FRIED BEEF BOURGUIGNON

Prep: 30 mins | Cook: 1 hour 30 mins | Serves: 6

Ingredients:

- 2 pounds beef chuck roast, cut into cubes (UK: 900g beef chuck roast, cut into cubes)
- Salt and pepper to taste
- 2 tablespoons olive oil (UK: 30ml olive oil)
- 4 slices bacon, chopped (UK: 4 slices bacon, chopped)
- 1 onion, chopped (UK: 1 onion, chopped)
- 2 cloves garlic, minced (UK: 2 cloves garlic, minced)
- 2 carrots, sliced (UK: 2 carrots, sliced)
- 2 stalks celery, sliced (UK: 2 stalks celery, sliced)
- 1 cup red wine (UK: 240ml red wine)
- 2 cups beef broth (UK: 480ml beef broth)
- 2 tablespoons tomato paste (UK: 30ml tomato paste)
- 1 teaspoon dried thyme (UK: 1 teaspoon dried thyme)
- 1 bay leaf

Instructions:

1. Preheat the Instant Pot Duo Crisp Air Fryer to 360°F (180°C) using the sauté function.

2. Season the beef chuck roast cubes with salt and pepper.

3. Heat olive oil in the Instant Pot inner pot. Add the chopped bacon and cook until crispy.

4. Add the seasoned beef cubes to the pot and cook until browned on all sides.

5. Stir in the chopped onion, minced garlic, sliced carrots, and sliced celery. Cook for another 5 minutes, until the vegetables are softened.

6. Pour in the red wine and beef broth, scraping the bottom of the pot to deglaze.

7. Stir in the tomato paste, dried thyme, and bay leaf.

8. Cover the Instant Pot with the lid and set the pressure cook function to high for 30 minutes.

9. Once the cooking cycle is complete, carefully release the pressure manually.

10. Remove the lid and switch to the air fry function. Set the temperature to 400°F (200°C).

11. Cook for an additional 20-30 minutes, until the sauce has thickened and the beef is tender.

12. Serve hot with mashed potatoes or crusty bread.

Nutritional Info: Calories: 450 | Fat: 20g | Carbs: 15g | Protein: 40g

12. AIR FRIED BEEF STROGANOFF

Prep: 15 mins | Cook: 40 mins | Serves: 4

Ingredients:

- 1 pound beef sirloin, thinly sliced (UK: 450g beef sirloin, thinly sliced)

- Salt and pepper to taste

- 2 tablespoons olive oil (UK: 30ml olive oil)

- 1 onion, sliced (UK: 1 onion, sliced)

- 8 ounces mushrooms, sliced (UK: 225g mushrooms, sliced)

- 2 cloves garlic, minced (UK: 2 cloves garlic, minced)

- 2 tablespoons all-purpose flour (UK: 30g all-purpose flour)

- 2 cups beef broth (UK: 480ml beef broth)

- 1 tablespoon Worcestershire sauce (UK: 15ml Worcestershire sauce)

- 1/2 cup sour cream (UK: 120g sour cream)

- Cooked egg noodles, for serving

Instructions:

1. Preheat the Instant Pot Duo Crisp Air Fryer to 400°F (200°C) using the sauté function.

2. Season the beef sirloin slices with salt and pepper.

3. Heat olive oil in the Instant Pot inner pot. Add the seasoned beef slices and cook until browned. Remove from the pot and set aside.

4. Add sliced onion and mushrooms to the pot. Cook until softened.

5. Stir in minced garlic and cook for another minute.

6. Sprinkle flour over the vegetables and cook, stirring constantly, for 1-2 minutes.

7. Slowly pour in beef broth and Worcestershire sauce, stirring to combine.

8. Return the cooked beef slices to the pot. Stir to combine.

9. Cover the Instant Pot with the lid and set the pressure cook function to high for 10 minutes.

10. Once the cooking cycle is complete, quick-release the pressure manually.

11. Stir in sour cream until well combined. Adjust seasoning with salt and pepper if needed.

12. Serve hot over cooked egg noodles.

Nutritional Info: Calories: 400 | Fat: 20g | Carbs: 20g | Protein: 35g

Instant Pot Duo Crisp Air Fryer Functions Used: Sauté, Pressure Cook

Certainly! Here are the next three recipes for beef main dishes using the Instant Pot Duo Crisp Air Fryer:

13. AIR FRIED MONGOLIAN BEEF

Prep: 20 mins | Cook: 15 mins | Serves: 4

Ingredients:

- 1 pound flank steak, thinly sliced against the grain (UK: 450g flank steak, thinly sliced against the grain)

- 1/4 cup cornstarch (UK: 30g cornstarch)

- 2 tablespoons vegetable oil (UK: 30ml vegetable oil)

- 3 cloves garlic, minced (UK: 3 cloves garlic, minced)

- 1 teaspoon fresh ginger, minced (UK: 1 teaspoon fresh ginger, minced)

- 1/2 cup soy sauce (UK: 120ml soy sauce)

- 1/2 cup water (UK: 120ml water)

- 1/4 cup brown sugar (UK: 50g brown sugar)

- 2 green onions, sliced (UK: 2 green onions, sliced)

- Sesame seeds, for garnish

Instructions:

1. In a bowl, toss the thinly sliced flank steak with cornstarch until well coated.

2. Preheat the Instant Pot Duo Crisp Air Fryer to 400°F (200°C) using the sauté function.

3. Add vegetable oil to the pot. Once hot, add the coated flank steak slices in a single layer.

4. Cook for 3-4 minutes, until browned and crispy. Remove the steak slices from the pot and set aside.

5. In the same pot, add minced garlic and ginger. Sauté for 1-2 minutes until fragrant.

6. Stir in soy sauce, water, and brown sugar. Cook until the sauce thickens slightly.

7. Return the cooked steak slices to the pot. Stir to coat them in the sauce.

8. Cover the Instant Pot with the lid and set the air fry function to 400°F (200°C).

9. Air fry for 5-7 minutes, until the sauce caramelizes and the beef is cooked through.

10. Garnish with sliced green onions and sesame seeds before serving.

Nutritional Info: Calories: 350 | Fat: 15g | Carbs: 20g | Protein: 30g

Instant Pot Duo Crisp Air Fryer Functions Used: Sauté, Air Fry

14. AIR FRIED BEEF ROULADEN

Prep: 30 mins | Cook: 1 hour | Serves: 4

Ingredients:

- 4 beef round steaks, thinly sliced (UK: 4 beef round steaks, thinly sliced)
- Salt and pepper to taste
- 4 slices bacon (UK: 4 slices bacon)
- 1 onion, thinly sliced (UK: 1 onion, thinly sliced)
- 4 dill pickles, halved lengthwise (UK: 4 dill pickles, halved lengthwise)
- 2 tablespoons Dijon mustard (UK: 30g Dijon mustard)
- 2 tablespoons vegetable oil (UK: 30ml vegetable oil)
- 2 cups beef broth (UK: 480ml beef broth)
- 2 tablespoons all-purpose flour (UK: 30g all-purpose flour)

Instructions:

1. Season each beef round steak with salt and pepper.
2. Lay a slice of bacon on each steak.
3. Place a few slices of onion and half of a dill pickle on top of the bacon.
4. Spread a thin layer of Dijon mustard over each steak.
5. Roll up each steak tightly, securing with toothpicks if necessary.
6. Preheat the Instant Pot Duo Crisp Air Fryer to 375°F (190°C) using the sauté function.
7. Add vegetable oil to the pot. Once hot, add the beef rouladen and cook until browned on all sides.
8. Pour beef broth into the pot and bring to a simmer.
9. Cover the Instant Pot with the lid and set the pressure cook function to high for 30 minutes.
10. Once the cooking cycle is complete, quick-release the pressure manually.
11. Remove the beef rouladen from the pot and set aside.
12. In a small bowl, mix flour with a little water to form a smooth paste.
13. Whisk the flour paste into the broth to thicken the gravy.
14. Return the beef rouladen to the pot and simmer for another 5-10 minutes.
15. Serve hot with mashed potatoes or spaetzle.

Nutritional Info: Calories: 400 | Fat: 20g | Carbs: 10g | Protein: 40g

Instant Pot Duo Crisp Air Fryer Functions Used: Sauté, Pressure Cook

15. AIR FRIED SALISBURY STEAK

Prep: 20 mins | Cook: 30 mins | Serves: 4

Ingredients:

- 1 pound ground beef (UK: 450g ground beef)
- 1/2 cup breadcrumbs (UK: 60g breadcrumbs)
- 1/4 cup milk (UK: 60ml milk)
- 1 egg, beaten (UK: 1 egg, beaten)
- 1 onion, finely chopped (UK: 1 onion, finely chopped)
- 1 tablespoon Worcestershire sauce (UK: 15ml Worcestershire sauce)
- Salt and pepper to taste
- 2 tablespoons vegetable oil (UK: 30ml vegetable oil)
- 2 cups beef broth (UK: 480ml beef broth)
- 2 tablespoons all-purpose flour (UK: 30g all-purpose flour)

Instructions:

1. In a bowl, combine ground beef, breadcrumbs, milk, beaten egg, chopped onion, Worcestershire sauce, salt, and pepper. Mix until well combined.

2. Shape the mixture into oval patties.

3. Preheat the Instant Pot Duo Crisp Air Fryer to 400°F (200°C) using the sauté function.

4. Add vegetable oil to the pot. Once hot, add the beef patties and cook until browned on both sides.

5. Remove the patties from the pot and set aside.

6. In the same pot, whisk together beef broth and flour until smooth.

7. Return the beef patties to the pot.

8. Cover the Instant Pot with the lid and set the pressure cook function to high for 15 minutes.

9. Once the cooking cycle is complete, quick-release the pressure manually.

10. Serve the Salisbury steak hot with mashed potatoes or rice, and spoon the gravy over the top.

Nutritional Info: Calories: 350 | Fat: 15g | Carbs: 15g | Protein: 35g

Instant Pot Duo Crisp Air Fryer Functions Used: Sauté, Pressure Cook

PORK AND LAMB MAIN DISHES

1. AIR FRIED PORK CHOPS

Prep: 10 mins | Cook: 20 mins | Serves: 4

Ingredients:

- 4 pork chops, bone-in (UK: 4 pork chops, bone-in)
- 2 tablespoons olive oil (UK: 30ml olive oil)
- 1 teaspoon paprika (UK: 1 teaspoon paprika)
- 1 teaspoon garlic powder (UK: 1 teaspoon garlic powder)
- 1 teaspoon onion powder (UK: 1 teaspoon onion powder)
- Salt and pepper to taste

Instructions:

1. Preheat the Instant Pot Duo Crisp Air Fryer to 400°F (200°C) using the air fry function.
2. Rub the pork chops with olive oil, paprika, garlic powder, onion powder, salt, and pepper.
3. Place the seasoned pork chops in the air fryer basket in a single layer.
4. Air fry for 10 minutes, then flip the pork chops.
5. Continue air frying for another 10 minutes, or until the pork chops reach an internal temperature of 145°F (63°C).
6. Serve hot with your favorite side dishes.

Nutritional Info: Calories: 280 | Fat: 15g | Carbs: 0g | Protein: 30g

Instant Pot Duo Crisp Air Fryer Functions Used: Air Fry

2. AIR FRIED BABY BACK RIBS

Prep: 15 mins | Cook: 1 hour 30 mins | Serves: 4

Ingredients:

- 2 racks baby back ribs (UK: 2 racks baby back ribs)
- 1 cup barbecue sauce (UK: 240ml barbecue sauce)
- 2 tablespoons brown sugar (UK: 30g brown sugar)
- 1 teaspoon garlic powder (UK: 1 teaspoon garlic powder)
- 1 teaspoon onion powder (UK: 1 teaspoon onion powder)
- Salt and pepper to taste

Instructions:

1. Remove the membrane from the back of the ribs, if necessary.

2. Season the ribs with salt, pepper, garlic powder, and onion powder.

3. Mix the barbecue sauce with brown sugar in a bowl.

4. Brush the ribs with the barbecue sauce mixture, reserving some for later.

5. Preheat the Instant Pot Duo Crisp Air Fryer to 300°F (150°C) using the air fry function.

6. Place the ribs in the air fryer basket, meat side down.

7. Air fry for 30 minutes, then flip the ribs and brush with more barbecue sauce.

8. Continue air frying for another 30-45 minutes, or until the ribs are tender and cooked through.

9. Serve hot with additional barbecue sauce on the side.

Nutritional Info: Calories: 450 | Fat: 25g | Carbs: 20g | Protein: 35g

Instant Pot Duo Crisp Air Fryer Functions Used: Air Fry

3. AIR FRIED PORK CARNITAS

Prep: 15 mins | Cook: 1 hour 30 mins | Serves: 6

Ingredients:

- 3 pounds pork shoulder, cut into chunks (UK: 1.4kg pork shoulder, cut into chunks)

- 1 onion, chopped (UK: 1 onion, chopped)

- 4 cloves garlic, minced (UK: 4 cloves garlic, minced)

- 1 teaspoon ground cumin (UK: 1 teaspoon ground cumin)

- 1 teaspoon dried oregano (UK: 1 teaspoon dried oregano)

- 1 teaspoon smoked paprika (UK: 1 teaspoon smoked paprika)

- Salt and pepper to taste

- 1/2 cup orange juice (UK: 120ml orange juice)

- 1/4 cup lime juice (UK: 60ml lime juice)

- 2 tablespoons vegetable oil (UK: 30ml vegetable oil)

Instructions:

1. Season the pork shoulder chunks with cumin, oregano, smoked paprika, salt, and pepper.

2. Preheat the Instant Pot Duo Crisp Air Fryer to 300°F (150°C) using the air fry function.

3. Add vegetable oil to the pot. Once hot, add the chopped onion and minced garlic. Sauté until softened.

4. Add the seasoned pork shoulder chunks to the pot and brown on all sides.

5. Pour in orange juice and lime juice.

6. Cover the Instant Pot with the lid and set the pressure cook function to high for 1 hour.

7. Once the cooking cycle is complete, quick-release the pressure manually.

8. Transfer the pork shoulder chunks to a baking sheet lined with parchment paper.

9. Shred the pork using two forks.

10. Place the shredded pork back into the Instant Pot and mix with the juices.

11. Set the Instant Pot Duo Crisp Air Fryer to 400°F (200°C) using the air fry function.

12. Air fry the pork carnitas for 15-20 minutes, stirring occasionally, until crispy.

13. Serve hot with tortillas, salsa, and your favorite toppings.

Nutritional Info: Calories: 350 | Fat: 20g | Carbs: 5g | Protein: 35g

Instant Pot Duo Crisp Air Fryer Functions Used: Sauté, Pressure Cook, Air Fry

4. AIR FRIED PORK FAJITAS

Prep: 20 mins | Cook: 15 mins | Serves: 4

Ingredients:

- 1 pound pork tenderloin, sliced (UK: 450g pork tenderloin, sliced)

- 1 onion, sliced (UK: 1 onion, sliced)

- 1 bell pepper, sliced (UK: 1 bell pepper, sliced)

- 2 tablespoons olive oil (UK: 30ml olive oil)

- 2 teaspoons chili powder (UK: 2 teaspoons chili powder)

- 1 teaspoon ground cumin (UK: 1 teaspoon ground cumin)

- 1 teaspoon smoked paprika (UK: 1 teaspoon smoked paprika)

- Salt and pepper to taste

- Tortillas, for serving

Instructions:

1. Preheat the Instant Pot Duo Crisp Air Fryer to 400°F (200°C) using the air fry function.

2. In a large bowl, toss the sliced pork tenderloin, onion, and bell pepper with olive oil, chili powder, cumin, smoked paprika, salt, and pepper.

3. Place the seasoned pork and vegetables in the air fryer basket.

4. Air fry for 12-15 minutes, or until the pork is cooked through and the vegetables are tender, stirring halfway through.

5. Serve the pork fajitas in tortillas with your favorite toppings.

Nutritional Info: Calories: 280 | Fat: 12g | Carbs: 15g | Protein: 25g

Instant Pot Duo Crisp Air Fryer Functions Used: Air Fry

5. AIR FRIED PULLED PORK

Prep: 15 mins | Cook: 1 hour 30 mins | Serves: 6

Ingredients:

- 3 pounds pork shoulder (UK: 1.4kg pork shoulder)
- 1 onion, sliced (UK: 1 onion, sliced)
- 4 cloves garlic, minced (UK: 4 cloves garlic, minced)
- 1 cup barbecue sauce (UK: 240ml barbecue sauce)
- 1/4 cup apple cider vinegar (UK: 60ml apple cider vinegar)
- 2 tablespoons brown sugar (UK: 30g brown sugar)
- 1 tablespoon Worcestershire sauce (UK: 15ml Worcestershire sauce)
- Salt and pepper to taste

Instructions:

1. Cut the pork shoulder into large chunks and season generously with salt and pepper.
2. Preheat the Instant Pot Duo Crisp Air Fryer to 300°F (150°C) using the air fry function.
3. Add the sliced onion and minced garlic to the pot and sauté until softened.
4. Add the seasoned pork shoulder chunks to the pot and brown on all sides.
5. In a bowl, mix together the barbecue sauce, apple cider vinegar, brown sugar, and Worcestershire sauce.
6. Pour the sauce mixture over the pork in the pot.
7. Cover the Instant Pot with the lid and set the pressure cook function to high for 60 minutes.
8. Once the cooking cycle is complete, quick-release the pressure manually.
9. Transfer the pork shoulder chunks to a cutting board and shred using two forks.
10. Return the shredded pork to the Instant Pot and mix with the sauce.
11. Set the Instant Pot Duo Crisp Air Fryer to 400°F (200°C) using the air fry function.
12. Air fry the pulled pork for 15-20 minutes, stirring occasionally, until crispy.
13. Serve the pulled pork on sandwiches or sliders with coleslaw, if desired.

Nutritional Info: Calories: 380 | Fat: 18g | Carbs: 20g | Protein: 35g

Instant Pot Duo Crisp Air Fryer Functions Used: Sauté, Pressure Cook, Air Fry

6. AIR FRIED BACON WRAPPED PORK TENDERLOIN

Prep: 20 mins | Cook: 40 mins | Serves: 4

Ingredients:

- 1 pork tenderloin (UK: 450g pork tenderloin)
- 8 slices bacon (UK: 8 slices bacon)
- 2 tablespoons olive oil (UK: 30ml olive oil)

- 2 cloves garlic, minced (UK: 2 cloves garlic, minced)

- 1 teaspoon dried thyme (UK: 1 teaspoon dried thyme)

- Salt and pepper to taste

Instructions:

1. Preheat the Instant Pot Duo Crisp Air Fryer to 400°F (200°C) using the air fry function.

2. In a small bowl, mix together olive oil, minced garlic, dried thyme, salt, and pepper.

3. Rub the pork tenderloin with the olive oil mixture.

4. Wrap the bacon slices around the pork tenderloin, securing with toothpicks if necessary.

5. Place the bacon-wrapped pork tenderloin in the air fryer basket.

6. Air fry for 35-40 minutes, or until the bacon is crispy and the pork reaches an internal temperature of 145°F (63°C).

7. Let the pork rest for 5 minutes before slicing.

8. Serve the bacon-wrapped pork tenderloin with your favorite sides.

Nutritional Info: Calories: 350 | Fat: 20g | Carbs: 1g | Protein: 35g

Instant Pot Duo Crisp Air Fryer Functions Used: Air Fry

Let me know if you need more recipes or any further assistance!

7. AIR FRIED SAUSAGE AND PEPPERS

Prep: 15 mins | Cook: 20 mins | Serves: 4

Ingredients:

- 1 pound Italian sausage links (UK: 450g Italian sausage links)

- 2 bell peppers, sliced (UK: 2 bell peppers, sliced)

- 1 onion, sliced (UK: 1 onion, sliced)

- 2 tablespoons olive oil (UK: 30ml olive oil)

- 1 teaspoon Italian seasoning (UK: 1 teaspoon Italian seasoning)

- Salt and pepper to taste

- Rolls or rice, for serving

Instructions:

1. Preheat the Instant Pot Duo Crisp Air Fryer to 375°F (190°C) using the air fry function.

2. In a bowl, toss the sliced bell peppers and onions with olive oil, Italian seasoning, salt, and pepper.

3. Place the sausage links in the air fryer basket.

4. Add the seasoned bell peppers and onions to the basket around the sausages.

5. Air fry for 18-20 minutes, flipping halfway through, until the sausages are cooked through and the vegetables are tender.

6. Serve the sausage and peppers in rolls as sandwiches or over rice.

Nutritional Info: Calories: 380 | Fat: 25g | Carbs: 10g | Protein: 25g

Instant Pot Duo Crisp Air Fryer Functions Used: Air Fry

8. AIR FRIED LAMB CHOPS

Prep: 10 mins | Cook: 15 mins | Serves: 2

Ingredients:

- 4 lamb loin chops (UK: 4 lamb loin chops)
- 2 tablespoons olive oil (UK: 30ml olive oil)
- 2 cloves garlic, minced (UK: 2 cloves garlic, minced)
- 1 teaspoon dried rosemary (UK: 1 teaspoon dried rosemary)
- Salt and pepper to taste

Instructions:

1. Preheat the Instant Pot Duo Crisp Air Fryer to 400°F (200°C) using the air fry function.

2. In a small bowl, mix together olive oil, minced garlic, dried rosemary, salt, and pepper.

3. Rub the lamb chops with the olive oil mixture.

4. Place the lamb chops in the air fryer basket.

5. Air fry for 12-15 minutes, flipping halfway through, until the lamb chops reach your desired level of doneness.

6. Serve the lamb chops with your favorite sides, such as roasted vegetables or mashed potatoes.

Nutritional Info: Calories: 400 | Fat: 30g | Carbs: 0g | Protein: 30g

Instant Pot Duo Crisp Air Fryer Functions Used: Air Fry

9. AIR FRIED LAMB KOFTA

Prep: 20 mins | Cook: 15 mins | Serves: 4

Ingredients:

- 1 pound ground lamb (UK: 450g ground lamb)
- 1 onion, grated (UK: 1 onion, grated)
- 2 cloves garlic, minced (UK: 2 cloves garlic, minced)
- 2 teaspoons ground cumin (UK: 2 teaspoons ground cumin)
- 1 teaspoon ground coriander (UK: 1 teaspoon ground coriander)
- 1/2 teaspoon ground cinnamon (UK: 1/2 teaspoon ground cinnamon)
- 1/4 teaspoon cayenne pepper (UK: 1/4 teaspoon cayenne pepper)
- Salt and pepper to taste

- Skewers, for grilling

Instructions:

1. Preheat the Instant Pot Duo Crisp Air Fryer to 375°F (190°C) using the air fry function.

2. In a bowl, mix together the ground lamb, grated onion, minced garlic, ground cumin, ground coriander, ground cinnamon, cayenne pepper, salt, and pepper.

3. Divide the mixture into equal portions and form them into sausage shapes around skewers.

4. Place the lamb kofta skewers in the air fryer basket.

5. Air fry for 12-15 minutes, turning halfway through, until the lamb kofta are cooked through and browned.

6. Serve the lamb kofta with tzatziki sauce and pita bread.

Nutritional Info: Calories: 350 | Fat: 25g | Carbs: 3g | Protein: 25g

Instant Pot Duo Crisp Air Fryer Functions Used: Air Fry

10. AIR FRIED LAMB SOUVLAKI

Prep: 20 mins | Cook: 15 mins | Serves: 4

Ingredients:

- 1 pound lamb leg or shoulder, cubed (UK: 450g lamb leg or shoulder, cubed)

- 1/4 cup Greek yogurt (UK: 60ml Greek yogurt)

- 2 tablespoons olive oil (UK: 30ml olive oil)

- 2 cloves garlic, minced (UK: 2 cloves garlic, minced)

- 1 teaspoon dried oregano (UK: 1 teaspoon dried oregano)

- Juice of 1 lemon (UK: Juice of 1 lemon)

- Salt and pepper to taste

- Pita bread, sliced tomatoes, onions, and tzatziki sauce, for serving

Instructions:

1. In a bowl, combine the Greek yogurt, olive oil, minced garlic, dried oregano, lemon juice, salt, and pepper to make the marinade.

2. Add the cubed lamb to the marinade and toss to coat evenly. Let it marinate for at least 1 hour or overnight in the refrigerator.

3. Preheat the Instant Pot Duo Crisp Air Fryer to 400°F (200°C) using the air fry function.

4. Thread the marinated lamb onto skewers.

5. Place the lamb skewers in the air fryer basket.

6. Air fry for 12-15 minutes, turning halfway through, until the lamb is cooked to your desired level of doneness and nicely browned.

7. Serve the lamb souvlaki with warm pita bread, sliced tomatoes, onions, and tzatziki sauce.

Nutritional Info: Calories: 300 | Fat: 15g | Carbs: 5g | Protein: 30g

Instant Pot Duo Crisp Air Fryer Functions Used: Air Fry

11. AIR FRIED LAMB MEATBALLS

Prep: 20 mins | Cook: 15 mins | Serves: 4

Ingredients:

- 1 pound ground lamb (UK: 450g ground lamb)

- 1/4 cup breadcrumbs (UK: 30g breadcrumbs)

- 1 egg, lightly beaten (UK: 1 egg, lightly beaten)

- 2 cloves garlic, minced (UK: 2 cloves garlic, minced)

- 2 tablespoons chopped fresh parsley (UK: 2 tablespoons chopped fresh parsley)

- 1 teaspoon ground cumin (UK: 1 teaspoon ground cumin)

- 1/2 teaspoon ground coriander (UK: 1/2 teaspoon ground coriander)

- Salt and pepper to taste

- Tzatziki sauce, for serving

Instructions:

1. In a large bowl, combine the ground lamb, breadcrumbs, beaten egg, minced garlic, chopped parsley, ground cumin, ground coriander, salt, and pepper. Mix until well combined.

2. Form the mixture into golf ball-sized meatballs.

3. Preheat the Instant Pot Duo Crisp Air Fryer to 375°F (190°C) using the air fry function.

4. Place the lamb meatballs in the air fryer basket in a single layer.

5. Air fry for 12-15 minutes, shaking the basket halfway through, until the meatballs are cooked through and golden brown.

6. Serve the lamb meatballs with tzatziki sauce for dipping.

Nutritional Info: Calories: 280 | Fat: 20g | Carbs: 5g | Protein: 20g

Instant Pot Duo Crisp Air Fryer Functions Used: Air Fry

12. AIR FRIED PORK SATAY

Prep: 30 mins | Cook: 15 mins | Serves: 4

Ingredients:

- 1 pound pork tenderloin, sliced into thin strips (UK: 450g pork tenderloin, sliced into thin strips)

- 1/4 cup coconut milk (UK: 60ml coconut milk)

- 2 tablespoons soy sauce (UK: 30ml soy sauce)

- 1 tablespoon brown sugar (UK: 15g brown sugar)

- 2 cloves garlic, minced (UK: 2 cloves garlic, minced)

- 1 teaspoon ground coriander (UK: 1 teaspoon ground coriander)

- 1/2 teaspoon ground turmeric (UK: 1/2 teaspoon ground turmeric)

- 1/4 teaspoon cayenne pepper (UK: 1/4 teaspoon cayenne pepper)

- Wooden skewers, soaked in water for 30 minutes

Instructions:

1. In a bowl, combine the coconut milk, soy sauce, brown sugar, minced garlic, ground coriander, ground turmeric, and cayenne pepper to make the marinade.

2. Add the sliced pork tenderloin to the marinade and toss to coat evenly. Let it marinate for at least 30 minutes in the refrigerator.

3. Preheat the Instant Pot Duo Crisp Air Fryer to 375°F (190°C) using the air fry function.

4. Thread the marinated pork strips onto the soaked wooden skewers.

5. Place the pork satay skewers in the air fryer basket.

6. Air fry for 12-15 minutes, turning halfway through, until the pork is cooked through and nicely browned.

7. Serve the pork satay with peanut sauce and steamed rice or noodles.

Nutritional Info: Calories: 280 | Fat: 12g | Carbs: 6g | Protein: 30g

Instant Pot Duo Crisp Air Fryer Functions Used: Air Fry

13. AIR FRIED PORCHETTA

Prep: 30 mins | Cook: 1 hour | Serves: 6

Ingredients:

- 2 pounds pork belly, skin on (UK: 900g pork belly, skin on)

- 1 tablespoon fennel seeds (UK: 15g fennel seeds)

- 2 tablespoons chopped fresh rosemary (UK: 30g chopped fresh rosemary)

- 2 tablespoons chopped fresh thyme (UK: 30g chopped fresh thyme)

- 4 cloves garlic, minced (UK: 4 cloves garlic, minced)

- Zest of 1 lemon (UK: Zest of 1 lemon)

- Salt and pepper to taste

Instructions:

1. Score the skin of the pork belly with a sharp knife in a crisscross pattern, being careful not to cut into the meat.

2. In a mortar and pestle, crush the fennel seeds until coarsely ground.

3. Mix together the crushed fennel seeds, chopped rosemary, chopped thyme, minced garlic, lemon zest, salt, and pepper to create the seasoning rub.

4. Rub the seasoning mixture all over the pork belly, ensuring it gets into the scored skin.

5. Roll up the pork belly tightly and tie it securely with kitchen twine at 1-inch intervals.

6. Preheat the Instant Pot Duo Crisp Air Fryer to 375°F (190°C) using the air fry function.

7. Place the rolled porchetta in the air fryer basket, seam side down.

8. Air fry for 45 minutes to 1 hour, or until the skin is crispy and the internal temperature reaches 160°F (71°C).

9. Remove the porchetta from the air fryer and let it rest for 10 minutes before slicing and serving.

Nutritional Info: Calories: 400 | Fat: 35g | Carbs: 2g | Protein: 20g

Instant Pot Duo Crisp Air Fryer Functions Used: Air Fry

14. AIR FRIED PORK BANH MI

Prep: 30 mins | Cook: 15 mins | Serves: 4

Ingredients:

- 1 pound pork loin, thinly sliced (UK: 450g pork loin, thinly sliced)

- 4 small baguettes or sandwich rolls, split (UK: 4 small baguettes or sandwich rolls, split)

- 1/4 cup mayonnaise (UK: 60g mayonnaise)

- 2 tablespoons Sriracha sauce (UK: 30ml Sriracha sauce)

- 1 tablespoon soy sauce (UK: 15ml soy sauce)

- 1 tablespoon rice vinegar (UK: 15ml rice vinegar)

- 1 tablespoon honey (UK: 15ml honey)

- 1 cup shredded carrots (UK: 150g shredded carrots)

- 1 cup thinly sliced cucumber (UK: 150g thinly sliced cucumber)

- 1/4 cup chopped fresh cilantro (UK: 30g chopped fresh cilantro)

- 4 tablespoons pickled daikon and carrot (optional) (UK: 60g pickled daikon and carrot)

Instructions:

1. In a small bowl, mix together the mayonnaise and Sriracha sauce to make the spicy mayo.

2. In another bowl, combine the soy sauce, rice vinegar, and honey. Add the sliced pork loin to the mixture and let it marinate for 15 minutes.

3. Preheat the Instant Pot Duo Crisp Air Fryer to 375°F (190°C) using the air fry function.

4. Remove the pork slices from the marinade and place them in the air fryer basket.

5. Air fry for 8-10 minutes, flipping halfway through, until the pork is cooked through and slightly caramelized.

6. Spread the spicy mayo on the split baguettes or sandwich rolls.

7. Layer the air-fried pork slices, shredded carrots, sliced cucumber, chopped cilantro, and pickled daikon and carrot on the baguettes.

8. Serve immediately, and enjoy your delicious pork banh mi sandwiches!

Nutritional Info: Calories: 450 | Fat: 20g | Carbs: 45g | Protein: 25g

Instant Pot Duo Crisp Air Fryer Functions Used: Air Fry

SEAFOOD MAIN DISHES

AIR FRIED SHRIMP

Prep: 15 mins | Cook: 10 mins | Serves: 4

Ingredients:

- 1 pound large shrimp, peeled and deveined (UK: 450g large shrimp, peeled and deveined)
- 1/2 cup breadcrumbs (UK: 60g breadcrumbs)
- 1/4 cup grated Parmesan cheese (UK: 25g grated Parmesan cheese)
- 1 teaspoon garlic powder (UK: 1 teaspoon garlic powder)
- 1 teaspoon paprika (UK: 1 teaspoon paprika)
- Salt and pepper to taste
- Cooking spray

Instructions:

1. Preheat the Instant Pot Duo Crisp Air Fryer to 400°F (200°C) using the air fry function.

2. In a shallow bowl, mix together breadcrumbs, grated Parmesan cheese, garlic powder, paprika, salt, and pepper.

3. Dip each shrimp into the breadcrumb mixture, coating it evenly on all sides.

4. Place the breaded shrimp in the air fryer basket, ensuring they are not overcrowded.

5. Spray the shrimp lightly with cooking spray.

6. Air fry for 8-10 minutes, flipping halfway through, until the shrimp are golden brown and cooked through.

7. Serve the air fried shrimp hot with your favorite dipping sauce.

Nutritional Info: Calories: 220 | Fat: 6g | Carbs: 16g | Protein: 24g

Instant Pot Duo Crisp Air Fryer Functions Used: Air Fry

AIR FRIED FISH STICKS

Prep: 15 mins | Cook: 12 mins | Serves: 4

Ingredients:

- 1 pound white fish fillets (such as cod or haddock), cut into strips (UK: 450g white fish fillets, cut into strips)

- 1/2 cup all-purpose flour (UK: 60g all-purpose flour)

- 2 eggs, beaten (UK: 2 eggs, beaten)

- 1 cup breadcrumbs (UK: 120g breadcrumbs)

- 1 teaspoon garlic powder (UK: 1 teaspoon garlic powder)

- 1 teaspoon dried dill (UK: 1 teaspoon dried dill)

- Salt and pepper to taste

- Cooking spray

Instructions:

1. Preheat the Instant Pot Duo Crisp Air Fryer to 375°F (190°C) using the air fry function.

2. In three separate bowls, place flour in one, beaten eggs in another, and breadcrumbs mixed with garlic powder, dried dill, salt, and pepper in the third.

3. Dip each fish strip into the flour, then into the beaten eggs, and finally into the breadcrumb mixture, coating evenly.

4. Place the breaded fish sticks in the air fryer basket, making sure they are not touching.

5. Spray the fish sticks lightly with cooking spray.

6. Air fry for 10-12 minutes, flipping halfway through, until the fish is golden brown and cooked through.

7. Serve the air fried fish sticks hot with tartar sauce or ketchup.

Nutritional Info: Calories: 280 | Fat: 7g | Carbs: 25g | Protein: 26g

Instant Pot Duo Crisp Air Fryer Functions Used: Air Fry

AIR FRIED FISH TACOS

Prep: 20 mins | Cook: 10 mins | Serves: 4

Ingredients:

- 1 pound white fish fillets (such as cod or tilapia), cut into strips (UK: 450g white fish fillets, cut into strips)

- 1/2 cup all-purpose flour (UK: 60g all-purpose flour)

- 2 eggs, beaten (UK: 2 eggs, beaten)

- 1 cup breadcrumbs (UK: 120g breadcrumbs)

- 1 teaspoon chili powder (UK: 1 teaspoon chili powder)

- 1 teaspoon ground cumin (UK: 1 teaspoon ground cumin)

- 1 teaspoon garlic powder (UK: 1 teaspoon garlic powder)

- Salt and pepper to taste

- 8 small corn or flour tortillas
- Shredded cabbage or lettuce, for serving
- Diced tomatoes, for serving
- Sliced avocado, for serving
- Lime wedges, for serving
- Fresh cilantro, for serving
- Hot sauce, for serving

Instructions:

1. Preheat the Instant Pot Duo Crisp Air Fryer to 375°F (190°C) using the air fry function.

2. In three separate bowls, place flour in one, beaten eggs in another, and breadcrumbs mixed with chili powder, ground cumin, garlic powder, salt, and pepper in the third.

3. Dip each fish strip into the flour, then into the beaten eggs, and finally into the breadcrumb mixture, coating evenly.

4. Place the breaded fish strips in the air fryer basket, making sure they are not touching.

5. Air fry for 8-10 minutes, flipping halfway through, until the fish is crispy and cooked through.

6. Meanwhile, warm the tortillas according to package instructions.

7. Assemble the tacos by placing some shredded cabbage or lettuce on each tortilla, followed by the air fried fish strips.

8. Top with diced tomatoes, sliced avocado, fresh cilantro, and a squeeze of lime juice.

9. Serve immediately with hot sauce on the side.

Nutritional Info: Calories: 320 | Fat: 8g | Carbs: 40g | Protein: 24g

Instant Pot Duo Crisp Air Fryer Functions Used: Air Fry

AIR FRIED COCONUT SHRIMP

Prep: 20 mins | Cook: 8 mins | Serves: 4

Ingredients:

- 1 pound large shrimp, peeled and deveined (UK: 450g large shrimp, peeled and deveined)
- 1/2 cup all-purpose flour (UK: 60g all-purpose flour)
- 2 eggs, beaten (UK: 2 eggs, beaten)
- 1 cup shredded coconut (UK: 120g shredded coconut)
- 1 cup Panko breadcrumbs (UK: 120g Panko breadcrumbs)
- Salt and pepper to taste

- Cooking spray

- Sweet chili sauce or mango salsa, for serving

Instructions:

1. Preheat the Instant Pot Duo Crisp Air Fryer to 375°F (190°C) using the air fry function.

2. In three separate bowls, place flour in one, beaten eggs in another, and a mixture of shredded coconut and Panko breadcrumbs in the third.

3. Season the shrimp with salt and pepper.

4. Dip each shrimp into the flour, then into the beaten eggs, and finally into the coconut breadcrumb mixture, pressing gently to adhere.

5. Place the breaded shrimp in the air fryer basket, ensuring they are not overcrowded.

6. Spray the shrimp lightly with cooking spray.

7. Air fry for 6-8 minutes, flipping halfway through, until the shrimp are golden brown and cooked through.

8. Serve the air fried coconut shrimp hot with sweet chili sauce or mango salsa for dipping.

Nutritional Info: Calories: 340 | Fat: 12g | Carbs: 32g | Protein: 24g

Instant Pot Duo Crisp Air Fryer Functions Used: Air Fry

AIR FRIED CRAB CAKES

Prep: 25 mins | Cook: 12 mins | Serves: 4

Ingredients:

- 1 pound lump crabmeat, drained and picked over (UK: 450g lump crabmeat, drained and picked over)

- 1/4 cup mayonnaise (UK: 60g mayonnaise)

- 1 large egg, beaten (UK: 1 large egg, beaten)

- 1 tablespoon Dijon mustard (UK: 1 tablespoon Dijon mustard)

- 1 tablespoon Worcestershire sauce (UK: 1 tablespoon Worcestershire sauce)

- 1 teaspoon Old Bay seasoning (UK: 1 teaspoon Old Bay seasoning)

- 1/4 cup chopped fresh parsley (UK: 15g chopped fresh parsley)

- 1/4 cup breadcrumbs (UK: 30g breadcrumbs)

- Salt and pepper to taste

- Cooking spray

- Lemon wedges, for serving

- Tartar sauce, for serving

Instructions:

1. In a large bowl, combine the lump crabmeat, mayonnaise, beaten egg, Dijon mustard, Worcestershire sauce, Old Bay seasoning, chopped parsley, breadcrumbs, salt, and pepper.

2. Gently mix until all ingredients are well combined.

3. Form the mixture into 8 crab cakes, shaping them firmly.

4. Preheat the Instant Pot Duo Crisp Air Fryer to 375°F (190°C) using the air fry function.

5. Spray the air fryer basket with cooking spray to prevent sticking.

6. Place the crab cakes in the air fryer basket, leaving space between each cake.

7. Air fry for 10-12 minutes, flipping halfway through, until the crab cakes are golden brown and cooked through.

8. Serve the air fried crab cakes hot with lemon wedges and tartar sauce on the side.

Nutritional Info: Calories: 190 | Fat: 8g | Carbs: 7g | Protein: 21g

Instant Pot Duo Crisp Air Fryer Functions Used: Air Fry

AIR FRIED FRIED CALAMARI

Prep: 15 mins | Cook: 10 mins | Serves: 4

Ingredients:

- 1 pound calamari rings, thawed if frozen (UK: 450g calamari rings, thawed if frozen)

- 1/2 cup all-purpose flour (UK: 60g all-purpose flour)

- 2 large eggs, beaten (UK: 2 large eggs, beaten)

- 1 cup Panko breadcrumbs (UK: 120g Panko breadcrumbs)

- 1/2 teaspoon garlic powder (UK: 1/2 teaspoon garlic powder)

- 1/2 teaspoon paprika (UK: 1/2 teaspoon paprika)

- Salt and pepper to taste

- Marinara sauce or aioli, for serving

Instructions:

1. Preheat the Instant Pot Duo Crisp Air Fryer to 375°F (190°C) using the air fry function.

2. Pat the calamari rings dry with paper towels to remove excess moisture.

3. In three separate bowls, place flour in one, beaten eggs in another, and a mixture of Panko breadcrumbs, garlic powder, paprika, salt, and pepper in the third.

4. Dip the calamari rings into the flour, then into the beaten eggs, and finally into the breadcrumb mixture, ensuring they are evenly coated.

5. Place the breaded calamari rings in the air fryer basket, making sure they are in a single layer.

6. Air fry for 8-10 minutes, shaking the basket halfway through, until the calamari rings are crispy and golden brown.

7. Serve the air fried calamari hot with marinara sauce or aioli for dipping.

Nutritional Info: Calories: 240 | Fat: 6g | Carbs: 26g | Protein: 20g

Instant Pot Duo Crisp Air Fryer Functions Used: Air Fry

AIR FRIED FRIED CATFISH

Prep: 15 mins | Cook: 12 mins | Serves: 4

Ingredients:

- 4 catfish fillets, about 6 ounces each (UK: 4 catfish fillets, about 170g each)
- 1 cup cornmeal (UK: 120g cornmeal)
- 1 teaspoon paprika (UK: 1 teaspoon paprika)
- 1/2 teaspoon garlic powder (UK: 1/2 teaspoon garlic powder)
- 1/2 teaspoon onion powder (UK: 1/2 teaspoon onion powder)
- Salt and pepper to taste
- Cooking spray
- Lemon wedges, for serving
- Tartar sauce, for serving

Instructions:

1. In a shallow dish, mix together the cornmeal, paprika, garlic powder, onion powder, salt, and pepper.
2. Pat the catfish fillets dry with paper towels.
3. Dredge each fillet in the cornmeal mixture, ensuring they are evenly coated on both sides.
4. Preheat the Instant Pot Duo Crisp Air Fryer to 400°F (200°C) using the air fry function.
5. Spray the air fryer basket with cooking spray.
6. Place the coated catfish fillets in the air fryer basket, leaving space between each fillet.
7. Air fry for 10-12 minutes, flipping halfway through, until the catfish is golden brown and cooked through.
8. Serve the air fried catfish hot with lemon wedges and tartar sauce on the side.

Nutritional Info: Calories: 280 | Fat: 4g | Carbs: 26g | Protein: 34g

Instant Pot Duo Crisp Air Fryer Functions Used: Air Fry

AIR FRIED FRIED COD

Prep: 20 mins | Cook: 10 mins | Serves: 4

Ingredients:

- 4 cod fillets, about 6 ounces each (UK: 4 cod fillets, about 170g each)

- 1 cup all-purpose flour (UK: 120g all-purpose flour)

- 2 large eggs, beaten (UK: 2 large eggs, beaten)

- 1 cup Panko breadcrumbs (UK: 120g Panko breadcrumbs)

- 1 teaspoon garlic powder (UK: 1 teaspoon garlic powder)

- 1 teaspoon paprika (UK: 1 teaspoon paprika)

- Salt and pepper to taste

- Cooking spray

- Lemon wedges, for serving

- Tartar sauce, for serving

Instructions:

1. Preheat the Instant Pot Duo Crisp Air Fryer to 400°F (200°C) using the air fry function.

2. Pat the cod fillets dry with paper towels.

3. Season the cod fillets with salt, pepper, garlic powder, and paprika.

4. Dredge each fillet in the flour, shaking off any excess.

5. Dip the floured fillets into the beaten eggs, allowing any excess to drip off.

6. Coat the fillets with the Panko breadcrumbs, pressing gently to adhere.

7. Spray the air fryer basket with cooking spray.

8. Place the coated cod fillets in the air fryer basket, leaving space between each fillet.

9. Air fry for 8-10 minutes, flipping halfway through, until the cod is golden brown and flakes easily with a fork.

10. Serve the air fried cod hot with lemon wedges and tartar sauce on the side.

Nutritional Info: Calories: 270 | Fat: 3g | Carbs: 26g | Protein: 35g

Instant Pot Duo Crisp Air Fryer Functions Used: Air Fry

AIR FRIED FRIED HALIBUT

Prep: 15 mins | Cook: 12 mins | Serves: 4

Ingredients:

- 4 halibut fillets, about 6 ounces each (UK: 4 halibut fillets, about 170g each)

- 1 cup breadcrumbs (UK: 120g breadcrumbs)

- 1/4 cup grated Parmesan cheese (UK: 25g grated Parmesan cheese)

- 1 teaspoon dried parsley (UK: 1 teaspoon dried parsley)

- 1/2 teaspoon garlic powder (UK: 1/2 teaspoon garlic powder)

- 1/2 teaspoon onion powder (UK: 1/2 teaspoon onion powder)

- Salt and pepper to taste

- Cooking spray

- Lemon wedges, for serving

- Tartar sauce, for serving

Instructions:

1. In a shallow dish, mix together the breadcrumbs, Parmesan cheese, dried parsley, garlic powder, onion powder, salt, and pepper.

2. Pat the halibut fillets dry with paper towels.

3. Dredge each fillet in the breadcrumb mixture, pressing gently to adhere.

4. Preheat the Instant Pot Duo Crisp Air Fryer to 400°F (200°C) using the air fry function.

5. Spray the air fryer basket with cooking spray.

6. Place the coated halibut fillets in the air fryer basket, leaving space between each fillet.

7. Air fry for 10-12 minutes, flipping halfway through, until the halibut is golden brown and flakes easily with a fork.

8. Serve the air fried halibut hot with lemon wedges and tartar sauce on the side.

Nutritional Info: Calories: 290 | Fat: 6g | Carbs: 23g | Protein: 35g

Instant Pot Duo Crisp Air Fryer Functions Used: Air Fry

AIR FRIED SALMON

Prep: 10 mins | Cook: 12 mins | Serves: 4

Ingredients:

- 4 salmon fillets, about 6 ounces each (UK: 4 salmon fillets, about 170g each)

- 2 tablespoons olive oil (UK: 30ml olive oil)

- 1 tablespoon lemon juice (UK: 15ml lemon juice)

- 1 teaspoon garlic powder (UK: 1 teaspoon garlic powder)

- 1 teaspoon paprika (UK: 1 teaspoon paprika)

- Salt and pepper to taste

- Lemon wedges, for serving

Instructions:

1. In a small bowl, whisk together the olive oil, lemon juice, garlic powder, paprika, salt, and pepper.

2. Brush the mixture over both sides of the salmon fillets.

3. Preheat the Instant Pot Duo Crisp Air Fryer to 400°F (200°C) using the air fry function.

4. Place the salmon fillets in the air fryer basket.

5. Air fry for 10-12 minutes, until the salmon is cooked through and flakes easily with a fork.

6. Serve the air fried salmon hot with lemon wedges on the side.

Nutritional Info: Calories: 320 | Fat: 20g | Carbs: 1g | Protein: 34g

Instant Pot Duo Crisp Air Fryer Functions Used: Air Fry

AIR FRIED TUNA STEAKS

Prep: 10 mins | Cook: 10 mins | Serves: 2

Ingredients:

- 2 tuna steaks, about 8 ounces each (UK: 2 tuna steaks, about 225g each)

- 2 tablespoons soy sauce (UK: 30ml soy sauce)

- 1 tablespoon sesame oil (UK: 15ml sesame oil)

- 1 tablespoon honey (UK: 15ml honey)

- 1 teaspoon grated ginger (UK: 1 teaspoon grated ginger)

- 1 teaspoon minced garlic (UK: 1 teaspoon minced garlic)

- 1/2 teaspoon red pepper flakes (optional) (UK: 1/2 teaspoon red pepper flakes)

- Sesame seeds, for garnish

- Sliced green onions, for garnish

Instructions:

1. In a small bowl, whisk together the soy sauce, sesame oil, honey, grated ginger, minced garlic, and red pepper flakes (if using).

2. Place the tuna steaks in a shallow dish and pour the marinade over them. Let them marinate for at least 10 minutes.

3. Preheat the Instant Pot Duo Crisp Air Fryer to 400°F (200°C) using the air fry function.

4. Remove the tuna steaks from the marinade and discard the excess marinade.

5. Place the tuna steaks in the air fryer basket.

6. Air fry for 8-10 minutes, depending on your desired level of doneness, flipping halfway through.

7. Serve the air fried tuna steaks hot, garnished with sesame seeds and sliced green onions.

Nutritional Info: Calories: 320 | Fat: 12g | Carbs: 10g | Protein: 42g

Instant Pot Duo Crisp Air Fryer Functions Used: Air Fry

AIR FRIED SCALLOPS

Prep: 15 mins | Cook: 8 mins | Serves: 4

Ingredients:

- 1 pound fresh scallops (UK: 450g fresh scallops)
- 2 tablespoons olive oil (UK: 30ml olive oil)
- 1 teaspoon paprika (UK: 1 teaspoon paprika)
- 1 teaspoon garlic powder (UK: 1 teaspoon garlic powder)
- Salt and pepper to taste
- Lemon wedges, for serving
- Chopped parsley, for garnish

Instructions:

1. Pat the scallops dry with paper towels.
2. In a small bowl, mix together the olive oil, paprika, garlic powder, salt, and pepper.
3. Brush the mixture over both sides of the scallops.
4. Preheat the Instant Pot Duo Crisp Air Fryer to 400°F (200°C) using the air fry function.
5. Place the scallops in the air fryer basket.
6. Air fry for 6-8 minutes, until the scallops are golden brown and cooked through.
7. Serve the air fried scallops hot with lemon wedges and chopped parsley.

Nutritional Info: Calories: 190 | Fat: 8g | Carbs: 5g | Protein: 25g

Instant Pot Duo Crisp Air Fryer Functions Used: Air Fry

AIR FRIED LOBSTER TAILS

Prep: 10 mins | Cook: 10 mins | Serves: 2

Ingredients:

- 2 lobster tails, about 6-8 ounces each (UK: 2 lobster tails, about 170-225g each)
- 2 tablespoons melted butter (UK: 30ml melted butter)
- 2 cloves garlic, minced (UK: 2 cloves garlic, minced)
- 1 tablespoon chopped fresh parsley (UK: 15ml chopped fresh parsley)
- Salt and pepper to taste
- Lemon wedges, for serving

Instructions:

1. Preheat the Instant Pot Duo Crisp Air Fryer to 400°F (200°C) using the air fry function.
2. Using kitchen shears, carefully cut through the top shell of each lobster tail.
3. Gently pull apart the shell, exposing the lobster meat, but keep the bottom part of the shell intact.
4. In a small bowl, combine the melted butter, minced garlic, chopped parsley, salt, and pepper.

5. Brush the butter mixture over the exposed lobster meat.

6. Place the lobster tails in the air fryer basket, shell side down.

7. Air fry for 8-10 minutes, until the lobster meat is opaque and cooked through.

8. Serve the air fried lobster tails hot with lemon wedges.

Nutritional Info: Calories: 180 | Fat: 8g | Carbs: 1g | Protein: 24g

Instant Pot Duo Crisp Air Fryer Functions Used: Air Fry

AIR FRIED OYSTERS

Prep: 15 mins | Cook: 8 mins | Serves: 4

Ingredients:

- 1 dozen fresh oysters, shucked (UK: 1 dozen fresh oysters, shucked)

- 1 cup all-purpose flour (UK: 120g all-purpose flour)

- 2 eggs, beaten (UK: 2 eggs, beaten)

- 1 cup breadcrumbs (UK: 120g breadcrumbs)

- 1 teaspoon garlic powder (UK: 1 teaspoon garlic powder)

- 1 teaspoon paprika (UK: 1 teaspoon paprika)

- Salt and pepper to taste

- Lemon wedges, for serving

- Tartar sauce, for dipping

Instructions:

1. Set up a breading station with three shallow bowls: one with flour, one with beaten eggs, and one with breadcrumbs mixed with garlic powder, paprika, salt, and pepper.

2. Dip each shucked oyster in the flour, then in the beaten eggs, and finally coat it in the breadcrumb mixture.

3. Preheat the Instant Pot Duo Crisp Air Fryer to 400°F (200°C) using the air fry function.

4. Place the breaded oysters in the air fryer basket in a single layer.

5. Air fry for 6-8 minutes, until the oysters are golden brown and crispy.

6. Serve the air fried oysters hot with lemon wedges and tartar sauce for dipping.

Nutritional Info: Calories: 220 | Fat: 6g | Carbs: 29g | Protein: 11g

Instant Pot Duo Crisp Air Fryer Functions Used: Air Fry

AIR FRIED FISH AND CHIPS

Prep: 20 mins | Cook: 20 mins | Serves: 4

Ingredients:

- 4 fillets of white fish (such as cod or haddock), skin removed (UK: 4 fillets of white fish, skin removed)
- 1 cup all-purpose flour (UK: 120g all-purpose flour)
- 1 teaspoon baking powder (UK: 1 teaspoon baking powder)
- 1 cup beer (UK: 240ml beer)
- Salt and pepper to taste
- 4 large potatoes, peeled and cut into thick fries (UK: 4 large potatoes, peeled and cut into thick fries)
- 2 tablespoons olive oil (UK: 30ml olive oil)
- Tartar sauce and lemon wedges, for serving

Instructions:

1. Preheat the Instant Pot Duo Crisp Air Fryer to 375°F (190°C) using the air fry function.
2. In a bowl, whisk together the flour, baking powder, salt, and pepper.
3. Gradually whisk in the beer until the batter is smooth.
4. Dip each fish fillet into the batter, allowing any excess to drip off.
5. Place the battered fish fillets in the air fryer basket, leaving space between each fillet.
6. In another bowl, toss the potato fries with olive oil, salt, and pepper until evenly coated.
7. Arrange the potato fries in a single layer in the air fryer basket alongside the fish.
8. Air fry for 15-20 minutes, flipping the fish halfway through cooking, until the fish is golden and crispy, and the fries are cooked through and crispy on the outside.
9. Serve the air fried fish and chips hot with tartar sauce and lemon wedges on the side.

Nutritional Info: Calories: 480 | Fat: 12g | Carbs: 58g | Protein: 30g

Instant Pot Duo Crisp Air Fryer Functions Used: Air Fry

SIDE DISHES

AIR FRIED MASHED POTATOES

Prep: 15 mins | Cook: 25 mins | Serves: 4

Ingredients:

- 4 large potatoes, peeled and diced (UK: 4 large potatoes, peeled and diced)
- 1/4 cup milk (UK: 60ml milk)
- 2 tablespoons butter (UK: 30g butter)
- Salt and pepper to taste

- Chopped chives or parsley for garnish (optional)

Instructions:

1. Place the diced potatoes in the Instant Pot inner pot and add enough water to cover them.

2. Close the lid, set the pressure release valve to "Sealing," and cook on high pressure for 8 minutes using the pressure cook function.

3. Once the cooking cycle is complete, perform a quick pressure release by turning the pressure release valve to "Venting."

4. Drain the potatoes and return them to the inner pot.

5. Add the milk, butter, salt, and pepper to the potatoes.

6. Mash the potatoes using a potato masher until smooth and creamy.

7. Transfer the mashed potatoes to a greased air fryer basket.

8. Spread the mashed potatoes evenly in the basket.

9. Air fry at 375°F (190°C) for 10-15 minutes, until the top is golden and slightly crispy.

10. Garnish with chopped chives or parsley if desired before serving.

Nutritional Info: Calories: 180 | Fat: 5g | Carbs: 30g | Protein: 4g

Instant Pot Duo Crisp Air Fryer Functions Used: Pressure Cook, Air Fry

AIR FRIED BAKED POTATOES

Prep: 5 mins | Cook: 45 mins | Serves: 4

Ingredients:

- 4 large baking potatoes (UK: 4 large baking potatoes)
- Olive oil
- Salt

Instructions:

1. Wash and scrub the potatoes thoroughly.

2. Poke each potato several times with a fork to create vents for steam to escape during cooking.

3. Rub each potato with olive oil and sprinkle with salt.

4. Place the potatoes directly on the air fryer basket or in the Instant Pot air fryer tray.

5. Air fry at 400°F (200°C) for 45-50 minutes, flipping halfway through, until the potatoes are tender when pierced with a fork and the skins are crispy.

6. Serve hot with your favorite toppings such as butter, sour cream, cheese, chives, and bacon bits.

Nutritional Info: Calories: 220 | Fat: 0.2g | Carbs: 51g | Protein: 5g

Instant Pot Duo Crisp Air Fryer Functions Used: Air Fry

AIR FRIED SWEET POTATO CASSEROLE

Prep: 20 mins | Cook: 30 mins | Serves: 6

Ingredients:

- 2 large sweet potatoes, peeled and diced (UK: 2 large sweet potatoes, peeled and diced)

- 1/4 cup brown sugar (UK: 50g brown sugar)

- 2 tablespoons butter, melted (UK: 30g butter)

- 1/4 teaspoon ground cinnamon

- 1/8 teaspoon ground nutmeg

- 1/4 cup chopped pecans (UK: 30g chopped pecans)

- Mini marshmallows, for topping

Instructions:

1. Steam the diced sweet potatoes in the Instant Pot using the steam function for 10 minutes or until tender.

2. Drain the sweet potatoes and transfer them to a mixing bowl.

3. Mash the sweet potatoes until smooth.

4. Add the brown sugar, melted butter, cinnamon, nutmeg, and chopped pecans to the mashed sweet potatoes. Mix until well combined.

5. Transfer the sweet potato mixture to a greased baking dish or air fryer-safe dish.

6. Top with a layer of mini marshmallows.

7. Air fry at 375°F (190°C) for 10-15 minutes, or until the marshmallows are golden brown and toasted.

8. Serve hot as a delicious side dish or dessert.

Nutritional Info: Calories: 180 | Fat: 7g | Carbs: 30g | Protein: 2g

Instant Pot Duo Crisp Air Fryer Functions Used: Steam, Air Fry

AIR FRIED POTATO GRATIN

Prep: 15 mins | Cook: 30 mins | Serves: 4

Ingredients:

- 4 large potatoes, thinly sliced (UK: 4 large potatoes, thinly sliced)

- 1 cup heavy cream (UK: 240ml heavy cream)

- 1 cup shredded Gruyere cheese (UK: 100g shredded Gruyere cheese)

- 1/4 cup grated Parmesan cheese (UK: 25g grated Parmesan cheese)

- 2 cloves garlic, minced

- 1 teaspoon fresh thyme leaves

- Salt and pepper to taste

- Cooking spray

Instructions:

1. Preheat the air fryer to 375°F (190°C).

2. In a mixing bowl, combine heavy cream, minced garlic, thyme leaves, salt, and pepper.

3. Layer the thinly sliced potatoes in the bottom of a greased baking dish.

4. Pour half of the cream mixture over the potatoes, then sprinkle with half of the Gruyere cheese.

5. Repeat the layers with the remaining potatoes, cream mixture, and Gruyere cheese.

6. Sprinkle the grated Parmesan cheese over the top layer.

7. Cover the baking dish with aluminum foil and place it in the air fryer basket.

8. Air fry for 25 minutes, then remove the foil and air fry for an additional 5 minutes, or until the potatoes are tender and the cheese is bubbly and golden brown.

9. Remove from the air fryer and let it rest for a few minutes before serving.

Nutritional Info: Calories: 350 | Fat: 22g | Carbs: 30g | Protein: 10g

Instant Pot Duo Crisp Air Fryer Functions Used: Air Fry

AIR FRIED ROASTED VEGETABLES

Prep: 10 mins | Cook: 20 mins | Serves: 4

Ingredients:

- 2 cups mixed vegetables (such as carrots, broccoli, cauliflower, bell peppers), cut into bite-sized pieces (UK: 300g mixed vegetables)

- 2 tablespoons olive oil

- 1 teaspoon garlic powder

- 1 teaspoon onion powder

- 1/2 teaspoon paprika

- Salt and pepper to taste

Instructions:

1. In a large mixing bowl, toss the mixed vegetables with olive oil, garlic powder, onion powder, paprika, salt, and pepper until evenly coated.

2. Preheat the air fryer to 375°F (190°C).

3. Spread the seasoned vegetables in a single layer in the air fryer basket.

4. Air fry for 15-20 minutes, shaking the basket halfway through, until the vegetables are tender and lightly browned.

5. Remove from the air fryer and serve immediately as a healthy and flavorful side dish.

Nutritional Info: Calories: 100 | Fat: 7g | Carbs: 10g | Protein: 2g

Instant Pot Duo Crisp Air Fryer Functions Used: Air Fry

AIR FRIED ROASTED POTATOES

Prep: 10 mins | Cook: 25 mins | Serves: 4

Ingredients:

- 1 lb baby potatoes, halved (UK: 450g baby potatoes, halved)
- 2 tablespoons olive oil (UK: 30ml olive oil)
- 2 teaspoons garlic powder
- 1 teaspoon paprika
- Salt and pepper to taste
- Chopped fresh parsley for garnish (optional)

Instructions:

1. Preheat the air fryer to 400°F (200°C).

2. In a large bowl, toss the halved baby potatoes with olive oil, garlic powder, paprika, salt, and pepper until evenly coated.

3. Place the seasoned potatoes in the air fryer basket in a single layer, making sure they are not overcrowded.

4. Air fry for 20-25 minutes, shaking the basket halfway through, until the potatoes are golden brown and crispy on the outside and tender on the inside.

5. Transfer the roasted potatoes to a serving dish, garnish with chopped fresh parsley if desired, and serve hot.

Nutritional Info: Calories: 180 | Fat: 7g | Carbs: 27g | Protein: 3g

Instant Pot Duo Crisp Air Fryer Functions Used: Air Fry

AIR FRIED FRENCH FRIES

Prep: 15 mins | Cook: 25 mins | Serves: 4

Ingredients:

- 4 large potatoes, peeled and cut into thin strips (UK: 4 large potatoes, peeled and cut into thin strips)
- 2 tablespoons olive oil
- 1 teaspoon garlic powder
- 1 teaspoon paprika
- Salt to taste

Instructions:

1. Soak the potato strips in cold water for about 30 minutes to remove excess starch. Then, drain and pat dry with paper towels.

2. Preheat the air fryer to 375°F (190°C).

3. In a large bowl, toss the potato strips with olive oil, garlic powder, paprika, and salt until evenly coated.

4. Arrange the seasoned potato strips in a single layer in the air fryer basket, making sure they are not overcrowded.

5. Air fry for 20-25 minutes, shaking the basket halfway through, until the fries are golden brown and crispy.

6. Transfer the fries to a serving dish and sprinkle with additional salt if desired.

7. Serve hot with your favorite dipping sauce.

Nutritional Info: Calories: 220 | Fat: 7g | Carbs: 36g | Protein: 4g

Instant Pot Duo Crisp Air Fryer Functions Used: Air Fry

AIR FRIED SWEET POTATO FRIES

Prep: 15 mins | Cook: 20 mins | Serves: 4

Ingredients:

- 2 large sweet potatoes, cut into fries (UK: 2 large sweet potatoes, cut into fries)

- 2 tablespoons olive oil (UK: 30ml olive oil)

- 1 teaspoon smoked paprika

- 1/2 teaspoon garlic powder

- 1/2 teaspoon onion powder

- Salt and pepper to taste

- Cooking spray

Instructions:

1. Preheat the air fryer to 400°F (200°C).

2. In a large bowl, toss the sweet potato fries with olive oil, smoked paprika, garlic powder, onion powder, salt, and pepper until well coated.

3. Place the seasoned sweet potato fries in the air fryer basket in a single layer, making sure they are not overcrowded.

4. Lightly spray the fries with cooking spray.

5. Air fry for 15-20 minutes, shaking the basket halfway through, until the sweet potato fries are crispy and golden brown.

6. Transfer the air-fried sweet potato fries to a serving plate and serve hot with your favorite dipping sauce.

Nutritional Info: Calories: 160 | Fat: 7g | Carbs: 24g | Protein: 2g

Instant Pot Duo Crisp Air Fryer Functions Used: Air Fry

AIR FRIED ONION RINGS

Prep: 15 mins | Cook: 10 mins | Serves: 4

Ingredients:

- 2 large onions, sliced into rings (UK: 2 large onions, sliced into rings)

- 1 cup all-purpose flour (UK: 120g all-purpose flour)

- 1 teaspoon garlic powder

- 1 teaspoon paprika

- Salt and pepper to taste

- 2 eggs, beaten

- 1 cup breadcrumbs (UK: 120g breadcrumbs)

Instructions:

1. Preheat the air fryer to 375°F (190°C).

2. In a shallow dish, combine the all-purpose flour, garlic powder, paprika, salt, and pepper.

3. Dip each onion ring into the flour mixture, shaking off any excess.

4. Dip the floured onion rings into the beaten eggs, then coat them with breadcrumbs.

5. Place the coated onion rings in a single layer in the air fryer basket, making sure they are not overlapping.

6. Air fry for 8-10 minutes, or until the onion rings are golden brown and crispy.

7. Serve hot as a delicious appetizer or side dish with your favorite dipping sauce.

Nutritional Info: Calories: 180 | Fat: 3g | Carbs: 33g | Protein: 6g

Instant Pot Duo Crisp Air Fryer Functions Used: Air Fry

AIR FRIED FRIED OKRA

Prep: 10 mins | Cook: 15 mins | Serves: 4

Ingredients:

- 2 cups fresh okra, sliced into rounds (UK: 300g fresh okra, sliced into rounds)

- 1 cup cornmeal (UK: 120g cornmeal)

- 1 teaspoon garlic powder

- 1 teaspoon paprika

- Salt and pepper to taste

- 2 eggs, beaten

Instructions:

1. Preheat the air fryer to 375°F (190°C).

2. In a shallow dish, combine the cornmeal, garlic powder, paprika, salt, and pepper.

3. Dip each okra slice into the beaten eggs, then coat them with the cornmeal mixture.

4. Place the coated okra slices in a single layer in the air fryer basket, making sure they are not overlapping.

5. Air fry for 12-15 minutes, flipping halfway through, until the okra is crispy and golden brown.

6. Serve hot as a crunchy and flavorful side dish or appetizer with your favorite dipping sauce.

Nutritional Info: Calories: 150 | Fat: 3g | Carbs: 28g | Protein: 5g

Instant Pot Duo Crisp Air Fryer Functions Used: Air Fry

AIR FRIED FRIED GREEN TOMATOES

Prep: 15 mins | Cook: 12 mins | Serves: 4

Ingredients:

- 2 large green tomatoes, sliced into 1/4-inch rounds (UK: 2 large green tomatoes, sliced into 0.5 cm rounds)

- 1 cup cornmeal (UK: 120g cornmeal)

- 1/2 cup all-purpose flour (UK: 60g all-purpose flour)

- 2 eggs, beaten

- 1 teaspoon garlic powder

- 1 teaspoon paprika

- Salt and pepper to taste

- Cooking spray

Instructions:

1. Preheat the air fryer to 375°F (190°C).

2. In a shallow dish, combine the cornmeal, all-purpose flour, garlic powder, paprika, salt, and pepper.

3. Dip each tomato slice into the beaten eggs, then coat them with the cornmeal mixture.

4. Place the coated tomato slices in a single layer in the air fryer basket, making sure they are not overlapping.

5. Lightly spray the coated tomato slices with cooking spray.

6. Air fry for 10-12 minutes, flipping halfway through, until the tomatoes are crispy and golden brown.

7. Transfer the fried green tomatoes to a serving plate and serve hot as a delicious appetizer or side dish.

Nutritional Info: Calories: 160 | Fat: 3g | Carbs: 29g | Protein: 5g

Instant Pot Duo Crisp Air Fryer Functions Used: Air Fry

AIR FRIED BRUSSELS SPROUTS

Prep: 10 mins | Cook: 15 mins | Serves: 4

Ingredients:

- 1 lb Brussels sprouts, trimmed and halved (UK: 450g Brussels sprouts, trimmed and halved)

- 2 tablespoons olive oil

- 2 cloves garlic, minced

- 1 teaspoon smoked paprika

- Salt and pepper to taste

- Grated Parmesan cheese for serving (optional)

Instructions:

1. Preheat the air fryer to 375°F (190°C).

2. In a large bowl, toss the Brussels sprouts with olive oil, minced garlic, smoked paprika, salt, and pepper until evenly coated.

3. Arrange the seasoned Brussels sprouts in a single layer in the air fryer basket.

4. Air fry for 12-15 minutes, shaking the basket halfway through, until the Brussels sprouts are crispy and browned on the edges.

5. Transfer the cooked Brussels sprouts to a serving dish and sprinkle with grated Parmesan cheese, if desired, before serving.

Nutritional Info: Calories: 120 | Fat: 7g | Carbs: 12g | Protein: 5g

Instant Pot Duo Crisp Air Fryer Functions Used: Air Fry

AIR FRIED FRIED CAULIFLOWER

Prep: 15 mins | Cook: 15 mins | Serves: 4

Ingredients:

- 1 head cauliflower, cut into florets (UK: 1 head cauliflower, cut into florets)

- 1 cup breadcrumbs (UK: 120g breadcrumbs)

- 1/2 cup grated Parmesan cheese (UK: 50g grated Parmesan cheese)

- 2 eggs, beaten

- 1 teaspoon garlic powder

- 1 teaspoon dried parsley

- Salt and pepper to taste

- Cooking spray

Instructions:

1. Preheat the air fryer to 375°F (190°C).

2. In a shallow dish, combine breadcrumbs, Parmesan cheese, garlic powder, dried parsley, salt, and pepper.

3. Dip each cauliflower floret into the beaten eggs, then coat them with the breadcrumb mixture.

4. Place the coated cauliflower florets in a single layer in the air fryer basket, making sure they are not overlapping.

5. Lightly spray the coated cauliflower florets with cooking spray.

6. Air fry for 12-15 minutes, flipping halfway through, until the cauliflower is tender and golden brown.

7. Transfer the fried cauliflower to a serving plate and serve hot as a crispy and flavorful side dish.

Nutritional Info: Calories: 180 | Fat: 6g | Carbs: 22g | Protein: 10g

Instant Pot Duo Crisp Air Fryer Functions Used: Air Fry

AIR FRIED FRIED ZUCCHINI

Prep: 10 mins | Cook: 12 mins | Serves: 4

Ingredients:

- 2 large zucchinis, sliced into rounds (UK: 2 large zucchinis, sliced into rounds)

- 1 cup breadcrumbs (UK: 120g breadcrumbs)

- 1/2 cup grated Parmesan cheese (UK: 50g grated Parmesan cheese)

- 2 eggs, beaten

- 1 teaspoon garlic powder

- 1 teaspoon dried oregano

- Salt and pepper to taste

- Cooking spray

Instructions:

1. Preheat the air fryer to 375°F (190°C).

2. In a shallow dish, combine breadcrumbs, Parmesan cheese, garlic powder, dried oregano, salt, and pepper.

3. Dip each zucchini round into the beaten eggs, then coat them with the breadcrumb mixture.

4. Place the coated zucchini rounds in a single layer in the air fryer basket, making sure they are not overlapping.

5. Lightly spray the coated zucchini rounds with cooking spray.

6. Air fry for 10-12 minutes, flipping halfway through, until the zucchini is tender and golden brown.

7. Transfer the fried zucchini to a serving plate and serve hot as a crispy and flavorful side dish.

Nutritional Info: Calories: 150 | Fat: 5g | Carbs: 20g | Protein: 8g

Instant Pot Duo Crisp Air Fryer Functions Used: Air Fry

AIR FRIED FRIED EGGPLANT

Prep: 15 mins | Cook: 15 mins | Serves: 4

Ingredients:

- 1 large eggplant, sliced into rounds (UK: 1 large eggplant, sliced into rounds)

- 1 cup breadcrumbs (UK: 120g breadcrumbs)
- 1/2 cup grated Parmesan cheese (UK: 50g grated Parmesan cheese)
- 2 eggs, beaten
- 1 teaspoon Italian seasoning
- Salt and pepper to taste
- Cooking spray

Instructions:

1. Preheat the air fryer to 375°F (190°C).
2. In a shallow dish, combine breadcrumbs, Parmesan cheese, Italian seasoning, salt, and pepper.
3. Dip each eggplant round into the beaten eggs, then coat them with the breadcrumb mixture.
4. Place the coated eggplant rounds in a single layer in the air fryer basket, making sure they are not overlapping.
5. Lightly spray the coated eggplant rounds with cooking spray.
6. Air fry for 12-15 minutes, flipping halfway through, until the eggplant is tender and golden brown.
7. Transfer the fried eggplant to a serving plate and serve hot as a crispy and flavorful side dish.

Nutritional Info: Calories: 160 | Fat: 6g | Carbs: 20g | Protein: 8g

Instant Pot Duo Crisp Air Fryer Functions Used: Air Fry

DESSERTS

1. AIR FRIED FRUIT CRISPS

Prep: 15 mins | Cook: 20 mins | Serves: 4

Ingredients:

- 4 cups mixed fresh or frozen fruits (such as apples, berries, peaches) (UK: 900g mixed fresh or frozen fruits)
- 1/4 cup granulated sugar (UK: 50g granulated sugar)
- 2 tablespoons all-purpose flour (UK: 30g all-purpose flour)
- 1/2 teaspoon ground cinnamon
- 1 cup old-fashioned rolled oats (UK: 100g old-fashioned rolled oats)
- 1/4 cup all-purpose flour (UK: 30g all-purpose flour)
- 1/4 cup brown sugar (UK: 50g brown sugar)
- 1/4 cup unsalted butter, melted (UK: 60g unsalted butter, melted)
- Vanilla ice cream, for serving (optional)

Instructions:

1. Preheat the air fryer to 375°F (190°C).

2. In a mixing bowl, combine the mixed fruits, granulated sugar, 2 tablespoons of flour, and ground cinnamon. Toss until the fruits are evenly coated.

3. Divide the fruit mixture among four individual ramekins or a baking dish.

4. In another bowl, mix together the rolled oats, 1/4 cup flour, brown sugar, and melted butter until crumbly.

5. Sprinkle the oat mixture evenly over the fruit in each ramekin or over the fruit in the baking dish.

6. Place the ramekins or baking dish in the air fryer basket.

7. Air fry for 18-20 minutes, or until the fruit is bubbly and the topping is golden brown.

8. Remove from the air fryer and let it cool for a few minutes before serving.

9. Serve warm, optionally topped with vanilla ice cream.

Nutritional Info: Calories: 280 | Fat: 9g | Carbs: 48g | Protein: 4g

Instant Pot Duo Crisp Air Fryer Functions Used: Air Fry

2. AIR FRIED APPLE PIE

Prep: 20 mins | Cook: 20 mins | Serves: 6

Ingredients:

- 1 package refrigerated pie crusts (2 crusts) (UK: 2 ready-made pie crusts)

- 4 cups thinly sliced apples (such as Granny Smith) (UK: 4 cups thinly sliced apples)

- 1/2 cup granulated sugar (UK: 100g granulated sugar)

- 2 tablespoons all-purpose flour (UK: 30g all-purpose flour)

- 1 teaspoon ground cinnamon

- 1/4 teaspoon ground nutmeg

- 1 tablespoon lemon juice

- 1 egg, beaten

- 1 tablespoon granulated sugar mixed with 1/2 teaspoon ground cinnamon, for topping

Instructions:

1. Preheat the air fryer to 375°F (190°C).

2. In a large bowl, combine the sliced apples, 1/2 cup granulated sugar, 2 tablespoons flour, ground cinnamon, ground nutmeg, and lemon juice. Toss until the apples are evenly coated.

3. Roll out one pie crust and line a pie dish with it. Trim any excess crust from the edges.

4. Pour the apple mixture into the prepared pie crust.

5. Roll out the second pie crust and place it over the filling. Trim any excess crust and crimp the edges to seal.

6. Brush the top crust with beaten egg and sprinkle with the cinnamon sugar mixture.

7. Cut several slits in the top crust to vent.

8. Place the pie dish in the air fryer basket.

9. Air fry for 18-20 minutes, or until the crust is golden brown and the filling is bubbly.

10. Remove from the air fryer and let it cool for a few minutes before serving.

Nutritional Info: Calories: 300 | Fat: 12g | Carbs: 47g | Protein: 3g

Instant Pot Duo Crisp Air Fryer Functions Used: Air Fry

3. AIR FRIED CHEESECAKE

Prep: 20 mins | Cook: 25 mins | Chill: 4 hours | Serves: 8

Ingredients:

- 1 1/2 cups graham cracker crumbs (UK: 150g graham cracker crumbs)

- 1/4 cup granulated sugar (UK: 50g granulated sugar)

- 1/2 cup unsalted butter, melted (UK: 115g unsalted butter, melted)

- 16 oz cream cheese, softened (UK: 450g cream cheese, softened)

- 1/2 cup granulated sugar (UK: 100g granulated sugar)

- 2 large eggs

- 1 teaspoon vanilla extract

- 1/4 cup sour cream (UK: 60g sour cream)

- 1 tablespoon all-purpose flour (UK: 15g all-purpose flour)

Instructions:

1. Preheat the air fryer to 325°F (160°C).

2. In a mixing bowl, combine the graham cracker crumbs, 1/4 cup granulated sugar, and melted butter. Press the mixture into the bottom of a 7-inch springform pan.

3. In another bowl, beat the cream cheese and 1/2 cup granulated sugar until smooth. Add the eggs, one at a time, beating well after each addition. Stir in the vanilla extract, sour cream, and flour until well combined.

4. Pour the cheesecake batter over the prepared crust in the springform pan.

5. Place the springform pan in the air fryer basket.

6. Air fry for 25 minutes, or until the edges are set but the center is still slightly jiggly.

7. Turn off the air fryer and let the cheesecake cool in the air fryer for 10 minutes.

8. Remove the cheesecake from the air fryer and cool completely on a wire rack.

9. Refrigerate the cheesecake for at least 4 hours or overnight before serving.

Nutritional Info: Calories: 380 | Fat: 28g | Carbs: 27g | Protein: 6g

Instant Pot Duo Crisp Air Fryer Functions Used: Air Fry

4. AIR FRIED BROWNIES

Prep: 15 mins | Cook: 20 mins | Serves: 9

Ingredients:

- 1/2 cup unsalted butter (UK: 115g unsalted butter)

- 1 cup granulated sugar (UK: 200g granulated sugar)

- 2 large eggs

- 1 teaspoon vanilla extract

- 1/3 cup unsweetened cocoa powder (UK: 40g unsweetened cocoa powder)

- 1/2 cup all-purpose flour (UK: 60g all-purpose flour)

- 1/4 teaspoon salt

Instructions:

1. Preheat the air fryer to 325°F (160°C).

2. In a microwave-safe bowl, melt the butter. Stir in the granulated sugar until well combined.

3. Add the eggs, one at a time, mixing well after each addition. Stir in the vanilla extract.

4. Sift the cocoa powder, all-purpose flour, and salt into the bowl. Mix until just combined.

5. Pour the brownie batter into a greased and lined 6-inch square baking pan.

6. Place the baking pan in the air fryer basket.

7. Air fry for 18-20 minutes, or until a toothpick inserted into the center comes out with moist crumbs.

8. Remove from the air fryer and let the brownies cool completely in the pan before slicing and serving.

Nutritional Info: Calories: 230 | Fat: 12g | Carbs: 30g | Protein: 3g

Instant Pot Duo Crisp Air Fryer Functions Used: Air Fry

5. AIR FRIED COOKIES

Prep: 15 mins | Cook: 10 mins | Serves: 12

Ingredients:

- 1/2 cup unsalted butter, softened (UK: 115g unsalted butter, softened)

- 1/2 cup granulated sugar (UK: 100g granulated sugar)

- 1/2 cup packed brown sugar (UK: 100g packed brown sugar)

- 1 large egg

- 1 teaspoon vanilla extract

- 1 1/2 cups all-purpose flour (UK: 180g all-purpose flour)

- 1/2 teaspoon baking soda
- 1/4 teaspoon salt
- 1 cup chocolate chips

Instructions:

1. Preheat the air fryer to 350°F (175°C).
2. In a mixing bowl, cream together the softened butter, granulated sugar, and brown sugar until light and fluffy.
3. Add the egg and vanilla extract, and beat until well combined.
4. In a separate bowl, whisk together the flour, baking soda, and salt.
5. Gradually add the dry ingredients to the wet ingredients, mixing until just combined.
6. Fold in the chocolate chips.
7. Scoop rounded tablespoons of dough onto a parchment-lined air fryer basket or tray, leaving space between each cookie.
8. Air fry for 8-10 minutes, or until the edges are golden brown.
9. Remove from the air fryer and let the cookies cool on a wire rack before serving.

Nutritional Info: Calories: 200 | Fat: 8g | Carbs: 30g | Protein: 2g

Instant Pot Duo Crisp Air Fryer Functions Used: Air Fry

6. AIR FRIED DONUTS

Prep: 15 mins | Cook: 10 mins | Serves: 8

Ingredients:

- 1 can (16.3 oz) refrigerated biscuits (UK: 1 can (400g) refrigerated biscuits)
- 1/4 cup granulated sugar (UK: 50g granulated sugar)
- 1 teaspoon ground cinnamon
- 2 tablespoons unsalted butter, melted (UK: 30g unsalted butter, melted)

Instructions:

1. Preheat the air fryer to 350°F (175°C).
2. Remove the biscuits from the can and separate them.
3. Use a small round cutter to cut out the center of each biscuit to form the donuts.
4. Place the donuts in the air fryer basket in a single layer, making sure they don't touch.
5. Air fry for 5 minutes, then flip the donuts over.
6. Air fry for an additional 3-5 minutes, or until the donuts are golden brown and cooked through.
7. In a shallow dish, mix together the granulated sugar and ground cinnamon.
8. Brush each donut with melted butter, then dip it into the cinnamon-sugar mixture until coated.

9. Serve warm and enjoy!

Nutritional Info: Calories: 180 | Fat: 7g | Carbs: 27g | Protein: 2g

Instant Pot Duo Crisp Air Fryer Functions Used: Air Fry

7. AIR FRIED CHURROS

Prep: 20 mins | Cook: 10 mins | Serves: 6

Ingredients:

- 1 cup water (UK: 240ml water)

- 2 tablespoons granulated sugar (UK: 25g granulated sugar)

- 1/2 teaspoon salt

- 2 tablespoons vegetable oil (UK: 30ml vegetable oil)

- 1 cup all-purpose flour (UK: 120g all-purpose flour)

- 1/4 cup granulated sugar (for coating) (UK: 50g granulated sugar)

- 1 teaspoon ground cinnamon (UK: 2g ground cinnamon)

- Vegetable oil spray

Instructions:

1. In a saucepan, combine water, 2 tablespoons sugar, salt, and 2 tablespoons vegetable oil. Bring to a boil over medium-high heat.

2. Reduce heat to low and stir in flour until the mixture forms a ball. Remove from heat and let cool for 5 minutes.

3. Transfer the dough to a piping bag fitted with a large star tip.

4. Pipe dough strips directly into the air fryer basket lined with parchment paper, cutting them to desired lengths with scissors.

5. Spray the churros with vegetable oil spray.

6. Air fry at 375°F (190°C) for 8-10 minutes, until golden brown and crisp.

7. In a shallow dish, mix together 1/4 cup granulated sugar and ground cinnamon.

8. Roll the hot churros in the cinnamon sugar mixture until coated.

9. Serve warm and enjoy!

Nutritional Info: Calories: 180 | Fat: 5g | Carbs: 31g | Protein: 2g

Instant Pot Duo Crisp Air Fryer Functions Used: Air Fry

8. AIR FRIED FRIED OREOS

Prep: 10 mins | Cook: 8 mins | Serves: 4

Ingredients:

- 1 cup pancake mix (UK: 120g pancake mix)

- 1/2 cup milk (UK: 120ml milk)

- 8 Oreo cookies

- Powdered sugar, for dusting (optional)

Instructions:

1. In a bowl, whisk together the pancake mix and milk until smooth.

2. Dip each Oreo cookie into the pancake batter, coating it completely.

3. Place the coated Oreos in a single layer in the air fryer basket.

4. Air fry at 370°F (187°C) for 4 minutes, then flip and air fry for an additional 4 minutes, until golden brown.

5. Remove from the air fryer and transfer to a plate.

6. Dust with powdered sugar if desired.

7. Serve warm and enjoy!

Nutritional Info: Calories: 250 | Fat: 10g | Carbs: 37g | Protein: 3g

Instant Pot Duo Crisp Air Fryer Functions Used: Air Fry

9. AIR FRIED BEIGNETS

Prep: 15 mins | Cook: 10 mins | Serves: 4

Ingredients:

- 1 cup all-purpose flour (UK: 120g all-purpose flour)

- 2 tablespoons granulated sugar (UK: 25g granulated sugar)

- 1 teaspoon baking powder (UK: 5g baking powder)

- 1/4 teaspoon salt

- 1/4 cup milk (UK: 60ml milk)

- 1 egg

- 1 tablespoon vegetable oil (UK: 15ml vegetable oil)

- 1 teaspoon vanilla extract (UK: 5ml vanilla extract)

- Powdered sugar, for dusting

Instructions:

1. In a bowl, whisk together the flour, sugar, baking powder, and salt.

2. In another bowl, whisk together the milk, egg, vegetable oil, and vanilla extract.

3. Combine the wet and dry ingredients until just mixed.

4. Transfer the dough to a floured surface and roll out to about 1/4 inch thickness.

5. Cut the dough into squares or circles.

6. Preheat the air fryer to 350°F (180°C).

7. Place the beignets in a single layer in the air fryer basket.

8. Air fry for 8-10 minutes, flipping halfway through, until golden brown and cooked through.

9. Remove from the air fryer and dust with powdered sugar.

10. Serve warm and enjoy!

Nutritional Info: Calories: 180 | Fat: 4g | Carbs: 31g | Protein: 4g

Instant Pot Duo Crisp Air Fryer Functions Used: Air Fry

10. AIR FRIED APPLE FRITTERS

Prep: 15 mins | Cook: 10 mins | Serves: 4

Ingredients:

- 2 cups all-purpose flour (UK: 240g all-purpose flour)

- 1/4 cup granulated sugar (UK: 50g granulated sugar)

- 1 tablespoon baking powder (UK: 15g baking powder)

- 1/2 teaspoon salt

- 1 teaspoon ground cinnamon (UK: 2g ground cinnamon)

- 2/3 cup milk (UK: 160ml milk)

- 2 large eggs

- 2 cups finely chopped apples (UK: 2 medium apples)

- Vegetable oil for frying

- Powdered sugar, for dusting

Instructions:

1. In a large bowl, whisk together the flour, sugar, baking powder, salt, and cinnamon.

2. In another bowl, whisk together the milk and eggs until well combined.

3. Gradually add the wet ingredients to the dry ingredients, stirring until just combined.

4. Fold in the chopped apples.

5. Preheat the air fryer to 350°F (180°C).

6. Scoop spoonfuls of the batter and drop them into the air fryer basket, leaving space between each fritter.

7. Air fry for 8-10 minutes, until golden brown and cooked through.

8. Remove from the air fryer and transfer to a paper towel-lined plate to drain excess oil.

9. Dust with powdered sugar.

10. Serve warm and enjoy!

Nutritional Info: Calories: 230 | Fat: 6g | Carbs: 40g | Protein: 5g

Instant Pot Duo Crisp Air Fryer Functions Used: Air Fry

11. AIR FRIED S'MORES

Prep: 5 mins | Cook: 5 mins | Serves: 4

Ingredients:

- 8 graham crackers
- 4 large marshmallows
- 4 squares of chocolate (milk or dark)
- 4 tablespoons chocolate hazelnut spread

Instructions:

1. Break the graham crackers in half to form squares.

2. Spread 1 tablespoon of chocolate hazelnut spread on 4 of the graham cracker squares.

3. Place a square of chocolate on top of each chocolate hazelnut spread-covered graham cracker.

4. Toast the marshmallows using the air fryer's broil function until golden brown and puffed, about 2-3 minutes.

5. Remove the marshmallows from the air fryer and place each one on top of a chocolate square.

6. Top each marshmallow with the remaining graham cracker squares to form sandwiches.

7. Serve immediately and enjoy the gooey goodness!

Nutritional Info: Calories: 200 | Fat: 6g | Carbs: 35g | Protein: 2g

Instant Pot Duo Crisp Air Fryer Functions Used: Broil

12. AIR FRIED BANANAS FOSTER

Prep: 5 mins | Cook: 8 mins | Serves: 2

Ingredients:

- 2 ripe bananas, sliced
- 2 tablespoons unsalted butter
- 1/4 cup brown sugar
- 2 tablespoons dark rum
- 1/2 teaspoon ground cinnamon
- Vanilla ice cream, for serving

Instructions:

1. Preheat the air fryer to 350°F (180°C).

2. In a small bowl, mix together the brown sugar and ground cinnamon.

3. Place the butter in the air fryer basket and melt it for 1-2 minutes.

4. Add the sliced bananas to the melted butter and toss to coat.

5. Sprinkle the brown sugar mixture over the bananas.

6. Air fry for 5-6 minutes, until the bananas are caramelized and softened.

7. Carefully add the rum to the air fryer basket and toss with the bananas.

8. Air fry for an additional 2 minutes to cook off the alcohol.

9. Serve the bananas foster over vanilla ice cream and enjoy!

Nutritional Info: Calories: 300 | Fat: 12g | Carbs: 45g | Protein: 2g

Instant Pot Duo Crisp Air Fryer Functions Used: Air Fry

13. AIR FRIED PEACH COBBLER

Prep: 10 mins | Cook: 25 mins | Serves: 6

Ingredients:

- 4 cups fresh or canned peaches, sliced

- 1 cup all-purpose flour

- 1 cup granulated sugar

- 1 teaspoon baking powder

- 1/2 teaspoon ground cinnamon

- Pinch of salt

- 1/2 cup unsalted butter, melted

- Vanilla ice cream, for serving

Instructions:

1. Preheat the air fryer to 350°F (180°C).

2. In a large bowl, combine the sliced peaches with 1/2 cup of sugar and the ground cinnamon. Mix well.

3. In another bowl, combine the flour, remaining 1/2 cup of sugar, baking powder, and salt. Mix until well combined.

4. Stir in the melted butter into the flour mixture until crumbly.

5. Spread the peach mixture evenly into the bottom of an air fryer-safe baking dish.

6. Sprinkle the crumbly flour mixture over the top of the peaches.

7. Air fry for 20-25 minutes, until the topping is golden brown and the peaches are bubbly.

8. Serve warm with a scoop of vanilla ice cream on top.

Nutritional Info: Calories: 320 | Fat: 14g | Carbs: 47g | Protein: 3g

Instant Pot Duo Crisp Air Fryer Functions Used: Air Fry

14. AIR FRIED CINNAMON ROLLS

Prep: 10 mins | Cook: 10 mins | Serves: 4

Certainly! Here are more dessert recipes for the Instant Pot Duo Crisp Air Fryer Cookbook:

15. Air Fried Fruit Empanadas

Prep: 20 mins | Cook: 12 mins | Serves: 8

Ingredients:

- 2 cups diced mixed fruit (such as apples, peaches, and berries)
- 1/4 cup granulated sugar
- 2 tablespoons all-purpose flour
- 1 teaspoon ground cinnamon
- 1 package refrigerated pie crusts (2 crusts)
- 1 egg, beaten
- 1 tablespoon water
- Powdered sugar, for dusting

Instructions:

1. Preheat the air fryer to 375°F (190°C).

2. In a bowl, combine the diced fruit, granulated sugar, flour, and cinnamon. Mix until the fruit is evenly coated.

3. Roll out the pie crusts on a lightly floured surface. Using a round cutter or a glass, cut out circles of dough.

4. Place a spoonful of the fruit mixture onto one half of each dough circle, leaving a small border around the edges.

5. Fold the dough over the filling to create a half-moon shape. Use a fork to crimp the edges and seal the empanadas.

6. In a small bowl, whisk together the beaten egg and water to make an egg wash.

7. Brush the tops of the empanadas with the egg wash.

8. Place the empanadas in the air fryer basket in a single layer, making sure they're not touching.

9. Air fry for 10-12 minutes, until the empanadas are golden brown and crisp.

10. Remove from the air fryer and let cool slightly before dusting with powdered sugar.

11. Serve warm and enjoy!

Nutritional Info: Calories: 220 | Fat: 9g | Carbs: 32g | Protein: 3g

Instant Pot Duo Crisp Air Fryer Functions Used: Air Fry

CLEANING AND MAINTAINING YOUR AIR FRYER

Keeping your Instant Pot Duo Crisp in top shape is essential for ensuring efficient, safe, and flavorful cooking for years to come. While this appliance is designed to be easy to clean and maintain, there are a few key steps you'll want to take to keep it running smoothly. In this chapter, we'll cover everything from properly cleaning the air fryer basket and pan to troubleshooting common issues and caring for your Duo Crisp according to the manufacturer's recommendations.

Cleaning the Air Fryer Basket

The air fryer basket is Ground Zero when it comes to cleaning your Instant Pot Duo Crisp. This perforated insert sees the most action, accumulating food particles, grease, and grime with each use. Proper and frequent cleaning is crucial to prevent buildup and ensure optimal air flow for perfectly crispy results.

The good news is, the air fryer basket is dishwasher safe, making cleanup a breeze. Simply remove it from the inner pot, give it a quick rinse to remove any loose debris, and then place it on the top rack of your dishwasher. The high heat and powerful water jets will ensure it comes out sparkling clean, ready for its next use.

If you don't have a dishwasher, no problem. You can easily hand wash the basket in hot, soapy water. Use a soft-bristled scrub brush or sponge to gently scrub away any stuck-on food or grease. Avoid using abrasive cleaners or scouring pads, as these can damage the non-stick coating.

Be sure to pay special attention to the perforations in the basket - this is where gunk and grease tend to accumulate the most. Use a toothpick or other small tool to carefully remove any debris that's built up in the holes. This will help maintain optimal air flow for perfectly crispy results.

After washing, make sure to rinse the basket thoroughly and allow it to air dry completely before placing it back in the inner pot. Any residual moisture can lead to rust or corrosion over time.

Cleaning the Air Fryer Pan

In addition to the basket, you'll also want to keep the air fryer pan itself clean and well-maintained. This is the stainless steel insert that sits inside the Duo Crisp's pressure cooker base, providing a sturdy surface for the basket to rest on.

Like the basket, the air fryer pan is dishwasher safe for easy cleaning. Simply remove it from the base, give it a quick rinse, and then pop it in the dishwasher. The high heat and powerful water jets will make quick work of any baked-on grease or food residue.

If washing by hand, use the same gentle approach as with the basket. Avoid abrasive cleaners or scouring pads, as these can damage the stainless steel surface. Instead, opt for a soft sponge or cloth and some warm, soapy water. Be sure to rinse the pan thoroughly and dry it completely before returning it to the Duo Crisp.

Preventing Grease Buildup Tips to prevent grease buildup

One of the keys to keeping your Instant Pot Duo Crisp in tip-top shape is preventing excess grease and oil from building up over time. This greasy buildup can not only lead to smoking and poor air flow, but it also increases the risk of fire and can be a real pain to clean.

To help prevent grease accumulation, there are a few simple steps you can take:

1. Use oil sparingly: When air frying, you only need a light coating of oil - often just a quick spritz of non-stick cooking spray is sufficient. Avoid dousing your food in excessive amounts of oil.
2. Blot excess oil: After cooking, use a paper towel or clean cloth to gently blot any excess oil or grease from the basket and pan. This will help keep the surfaces clean.
3. Clean after each use: Make a habit of cleaning the air fryer basket and pan after every use. Don't let that grease and grime sit and bake on.
4. Descale regularly: Over time, mineral deposits from water and cooked-on oils can build up on the heating element and interior surfaces. Regularly descaling your Duo Crisp will help prevent this.

Descaling Your Air Fryer- How to descale the fryer

Just like your coffee maker or other kitchen appliances, the Instant Pot Duo Crisp needs to be descaled periodically to remove mineral buildup and keep it running at peak efficiency.

The frequency of descaling will depend on how often you use your Duo Crisp, as well as the mineral content of your local water supply. As a general rule of thumb, most manufacturers recommend descaling every 3-6 months for regular home use.

Here's how to descale your Instant Pot Duo Crisp:

Supplies Needed:

- White vinegar or a commercial descaling solution
- A long, narrow cleaning brush (optional)

Instructions:

1. Unplug the Duo Crisp and allow it to cool completely.
2. Remove the inner pot, air fryer basket, and any other accessories.
3. In a measuring cup, mix equal parts white vinegar and water, or use a commercial descaling solution. You'll need enough liquid to fill the inner pot to the "PC MAX - 2/3" line.
4. Pour the descaling solution into the pressure cooker base, being careful not to get any liquid on the control panel or air fryer lid.
5. Place the inner pot back into the base and close the air fryer lid.
6. Select the "Steam" function and set the time for 5 minutes.
7. Once the cycle is complete, allow the pressure to release naturally.
8. Carefully remove the inner pot and dispose of the used descaling solution.
9. Use a long, narrow cleaning brush to gently scrub the interior of the pressure cooker base, focusing on the heating element and any mineral buildup.
10. Rinse the base thoroughly with clean water to remove any remaining residue.
11. Dry all surfaces completely before reassembling the Duo Crisp.

If you notice a significant amount of scale or mineral buildup, you may need to repeat the descaling process a few times to fully remove it. Additionally, if you live in an area with particularly hard water, you may need to descale more frequently.

Replacing Accessories- When to replace accessories

While the Instant Pot Duo Crisp is built to last, the various accessories and components will eventually need to be replaced over time. Keep an eye out for any signs of wear, damage, or deterioration, and replace these items as needed for optimal performance and safety.

Some key items to watch out for include:

Air Fryer Basket: Over time, the non-stick coating on the basket may start to wear down, leading to increased sticking and decreased air flow. Replace the basket if you notice significant scratching or flaking.

Silicone Sealing Ring: The sealing ring that creates the airtight seal for pressure cooking is subject to wear and tear. Replace it every 12-18 months, or if you notice any cracking, warping, or loss of flexibility.

Float Valve: The float valve that indicates pressure in the pot can become stuck or worn down, preventing proper pressure release. Check it regularly and replace if needed.

Power Cord: Inspect the power cord for any signs of damage, fraying, or wear. If the cord appears compromised in any way, discontinue use and order a replacement.

When it comes time to replace any of these components, be sure to source genuine Instant Pot-branded accessories. Using third-party or off-brand items may not provide the same level of fit, function, and safety.

Troubleshooting Common Problems

Even with proper care and maintenance, you may occasionally run into issues with your Instant Pot Duo Crisp. Here are some of the most common problems you might encounter, along with solutions to get you back up and running:

Air Fryer Lid Won't Turn On:

- Check the connection between the lid and the pressure cooker base to ensure it's secure.
- Inspect the power cord for any damage or loose connections.
- If the microswitch that activates the lid is seized up with grease or damaged, contact customer service.

Black Smoke from the Air Fryer Lid:

- Try using a different oil with a higher smoke point, like avocado or canola oil.
- Check for any food residue or grease buildup on the bottom of the inner pot or around the heating element.
- If the issue persists, discontinue use and contact customer service.

White Smoke from the Air Fryer Lid:

- Cooking foods with a high fat content, like bacon or sausage, can cause white smoke as the fat vaporizes.
- Make sure to pat dry any moist foods before air frying to prevent excess steam.
- Avoid letting seasoning or breading blow onto the heating element.

Difficulty Closing the Pressure Cooking Lid:

- Ensure the sealing ring is properly installed and not obstructing the lid.
- Check that the float valve is down before attempting to close the lid.
- Allow the contents in the inner pot to cool slightly before closing the lid.

Difficulty Opening the Pressure Cooking Lid:

- Make sure all pressure has been fully released before attempting to open the lid.
- If the float valve is stuck, gently press down on it with a long utensil.
- Inspect the float valve and surrounding area for any food debris or residue.

Stuck Inner Pot:

- The cooling of the inner pot can sometimes create a slight vacuum, causing it to adhere to the lid.
- Press the quick release button to release any remaining pressure before opening.

In the rare event you encounter an error code or other issue you can't resolve, don't hesitate to reach out to Instant Pot's customer service team. They have a wealth of experience troubleshooting all kinds of problems and can provide expert guidance to get you back to pressure cooking and air frying in no time.

Storing Your Instant Pot Duo Crisp- Storing tips

When not in use, proper storage of your Instant Pot Duo Crisp is key to keeping it in top shape. Start by ensuring all accessories are thoroughly cleaned and dried. Then, carefully nest the inner pot, air fryer basket, and other removable parts inside the pressure cooker base.

Next, place the pressure cooking lid on top, making sure the steam release valve is in the "Venting" position. This will help prevent any potential damage to the valve. Finally, place the air fryer lid on top of the pressure cooking lid and secure the protective silicone pad underneath.

It's best to store your Duo Crisp on the countertop or in a cabinet, rather than in a drawer where the components could get jostled around. Avoid placing heavy items on top of the appliance, as this could potentially warp or damage the lids.

When it comes time to use your Duo Crisp again, simply unpack it, give the inner pot and accessories a quick rinse, and you'll be ready to pressure cook, air fry, and more. With proper care and storage, your Instant Pot will provide years of reliable, hassle-free performance.

Manufacturer Care Recommendations

In addition to the cleaning and maintenance tips outlined in this chapter, it's important to follow the specific care and use recommendations provided by the manufacturer, Instant Brands.

According to the Instant Pot Duo Crisp user manual, there are a few key points to keep in mind:

- Always use an Instant Pot stainless steel inner pot when using the Air Fryer Lid. Do not use a ceramic coated inner pot.
- Before each use, check the steam release valve/handle, steam release pipe, anti-block shield, and float valve for any clogging or debris.
- Do not submerge the cooker base or air fryer lid in water or rinse them under the tap. Wipe them down with a damp cloth instead.
- Regularly inspect the power cord and plug for any damage. Discontinue use if issues are found.
- When storing, leave the pressure cooking lid loosely on the cooker base with the steam release valve in the "Venting" position.
- Avoid using the appliance if it has been dropped or appears damaged in any way. Contact customer service for assistance.

By following these manufacturer guidelines, along with the cleaning and maintenance advice outlined earlier in this chapter, you can help ensure your Instant Pot Duo Crisp delivers years of reliable, safe, and delicious performance in your kitchen.

Caring for your Instant Pot Duo Crisp doesn't have to be a chore. With a little bit of routine attention, you can keep this amazing multi-cooker in tip-top shape, ready to whip up countless meals at a moment's notice. So roll up your sleeves, get cleaning, and enjoy the fruits of your labor - or should I say, the fruits of your sparkling, well-maintained air fryer!

CONCLUSION

Congratulations! By now, you've learned all the essential ins and outs of your Instant Pot Duo Crisp, from its powerful pressure cooking and air frying capabilities to the proper care and maintenance required to keep it running at its best. Whether you're a seasoned Instant Pot pro or a complete newcomer to this revolutionary appliance, I hope this cookbook has equipped you with the knowledge and recipes to make the most of your Duo Crisp.

Throughout these pages, we've covered a wide range of topics to ensure you feel confident and empowered in the kitchen. We started with an overview of the Duo Crisp's key features and benefits, highlighting how its unique combination of pressure cooking and air frying can streamline your meal prep and unlock a world of culinary possibilities.

Then, we dove into the nitty-gritty of getting your new appliance set up and ready for action. From unpacking and assembling the various components to performing that all-important initial test run, you now have a solid grasp of how to properly establish your Duo Crisp for safe and effective use.

Of course, no Instant Pot cookbook would be complete without a deep dive into essential accessories and tools. We explored a variety of must-have items - from air fryer basket liners and steamer baskets to silicone mitts and meat thermometers - that can take your Duo Crisp cooking to the next level. Armed with the right equipment, you'll be whipping up restaurant-quality meals in no time.

And speaking of meals, the heart of this cookbook lies in the extensive collection of delectable recipes we covered. From crowd-pleasing appetizers and snacks to flavor-packed main dishes and decadent desserts, we left no culinary stone unturned. Whether you're in the mood for crispy, golden-brown air fried favorites or tender, fall-off-the-bone pressure cooked delights, this book has something to satisfy every craving.

But we didn't stop there. In the final chapter, we tackled the important topic of cleaning and maintaining your Instant Pot Duo Crisp. After all, proper care is essential for ensuring this appliance delivers reliable, long-lasting performance. From detailed instructions on cleaning the air fryer basket and pan to tips for preventing grease buildup and troubleshooting common issues, you're now equipped with the knowledge to keep your Duo Crisp in tip-top shape.

As we reach the end of this cookbook, I hope you feel inspired, empowered, and eager to put your Instant Pot Duo Crisp to work in your own kitchen. This truly is a revolutionary appliance that can transform the way you approach meal prep, cooking, and entertaining. With its unparalleled versatility and user-friendly design, the possibilities are endless.

Of course, the learning process doesn't have to end here. Instant Brands, the manufacturer of the Duo Crisp, offers a wealth of additional resources to help you get the most out of your appliance. Be sure to visit their website at instantpot.com for access to instructional videos, recipe ideas, and a thriving community of fellow Instant Pot enthusiasts. You can also reach out to their customer service team with any questions or concerns that arise.

As you continue on your Instant Pot journey, remember to have fun and experiment. Don't be afraid to try new recipes, explore different cooking techniques, and find creative ways to incorporate the Duo Crisp into your culinary repertoire. That's half the joy of owning this remarkable appliance - the opportunity to discover endless delicious possibilities.

So what are you waiting for? Go forth, fire up your Instant Pot Duo Crisp, and get cooking! Whether you're whipping up a quick weeknight dinner, hosting a crowd-pleasing game day spread, or indulging in a decadent dessert, this trusty multi-cooker will have your back every step of the way. Enjoy the process, savor the flavors, and revel in the convenience of Instant Pot cooking. Happy cooking!

Printed in Great Britain
by Amazon